D1571469

THE INFINITE EMOTIONS OF COFFEE

Alon Y. Halevy

Dear Mr. Clarke,

We hope you will enjoy these tales from around the world &

Diana & Alon

Macchiatone Communications, LLC
California

Published in the United States by Macchiatone Communications, LLC

Library of Congress Cataloging-in-Publication data
    Halevy, Alon
    The Infinite Emotions of Coffee/ Alon Halevy. -1st ed.

ISBN 978-0-9847715-0-9

2011010494

Printed in the United States of America

First edition: December 2011

Editor: Oriana Li Halevy

Design & Production: Amanda N. Wilson

www.macchiatone.com

CONTENTS

PREFACE

I HAD BEEN SEARCHING FOR THE PERFECT ESPRESSO DRINK for a very long time when it finally revealed itself to me at Caffe Del Doge (now Café Venetia) in Palo Alto, California. After many visits there, I managed to work up the nerve to point out that their cappuccinos, though prepared with the utmost Italian artistry, were too milky for my palate. The barista suggested I try a *macchiatone*. With more milk than a macchiato but less than a cappuccino, the macchiatone struck just the right balance between foamed milk and espresso, forming a sublime drink.

Excited by my discovery, I blogged about the macchiatone that same day. To my surprise, when I googled "macchiatone" a week later, my blog post came up as the first result. In today's Web-powered universe, this meant that the macchiatone was virtually unknown to the world. My subsequent experiences confirmed that observation.

Kasper Halevy packing the perfect portafilter.

Over the next few months, my professional travels took me to New Zealand, Vietnam, Israel, the Czech Republic, and other far-flung places. I found myself trying to explain to the local baristas how to make the macchiatone. Through the diverse reactions I received and the different café experiences I had, the richness and complexity of world coffee cultures captivated me and raised many questions in my mind. As I continued on my odyssey, the idea of writing a book to share my discoveries dawned on me.

I was not born into the world of cappuccinos and macchiatones, although both of my children, Karina and Kasper, will proudly tell you that their first four-syllable word was "*cappuccino*." My first brush with coffee was at the age of two. Elated to have a grandson after five granddaughters, my Greek-born grandfather delighted in cementing our special bond by putting me on his lap and letting me sip from his cups of scalding Turkish coffee.

Things went downhill after that. I spent my formative teenage years drinking instant coffee (two teaspoons of sugar graced each cup), and even formed a ritual around preparing the tasteless brew during my service in the Israeli military. My misguided love for instant coffee was followed by a fascination with American drip coffee, which kept me sufficiently caffeinated to earn a Ph.D. in Computer Science from Stanford University in 1993.

I had my first encounter with an espresso machine in 1993 when I was working at AT&T Bell Labs in Murray Hill, New Jersey and some coffee connoisseurs in the office were having beans shipped from Peet's Coffee. Founded in the 1960's in Berkeley, California, Peet's was the first roaster to produce a high quality espresso roast and ship them to coffee lovers across the country.

A few years later, after my stint in New Jersey reaffirmed my affinity for the West Coast, I became a professor of Computer Science at the University of Washington in Seattle. It soon became clear that if I were to succeed in the coffee capital of the U.S., I needed to raise my coffee vocabulary and skills up a notch or two. In fact, I spent the first year on the job learning how to order coffee effectively in Seattle cafés, finally perfecting the phrase "two percent double half-caf wet cappuccino." The caffeine clearly worked, as I managed to mentor a few Ph.D. students who later became stars in my field, while collecting some international recognition for myself in the process, including the Presidential Early Career Award for Scientists and Engineers from President Bill Clinton.

As a computer science professor I naturally dabbled in entrepreneurial activities. One of those activities ultimately led me to take a break from academia and join Google. The move to Google headquarters in Mountain View, California prompted yet another step up on the coffee ladder.

Googlers take coffee very seriously. Thousands of world-class engineers, pure perfectionists when it comes to software, also spare no effort in achieving the perfect cuppa. Understanding the importance of caffeine to its bottom line, Google provides unrivaled experiential spaces to explore and develop one's barista skills.

My current job as leader of the Database Research Group at Google involves extensive travel to many parts of the world for speaking engagements about my group's work. During these trips, I have had the good fortune of sampling coffees and exploring the many cultural aspects of coffee. I have inhaled, witnessed, and experienced coffee as a catalyst of social interaction, a beverage of choice at moments of respite in business settings, a stimulant that invigorates idea creation and live exchange, and an alluring magnet that pulls people of multiple cultures and disparate backgrounds together. The purpose of this book is to bring all these facets of coffee to life through a collection of vignettes, photographs, and even diagrams to convey the infinite emotions of coffee.

I visit cafés that have special stories to tell, others that carry historical significance, and some that are simply too charming to ignore. I visit coffee farms in South and Central America and in Ethiopia, the birthplace of coffee, witnessing the lives of the people who are responsible for our daily delights. I discover how coffee culture is being radically transformed throughout the world and expanding its seductive spheres of influence. I visit some of the fabulous people who are responsible for this transformation, including growers, importers, roasters, baristas, and a few odd characters. Some of these baristas are part of a fascinating subculture of barista championships that has taken coffee to a completely new level as a competitive sport.

While this is not intended to be a book about coffee history, I cover some of the highlights of history, or legend, as it often turns out to be. I try to shed some light on the Italian passion for and romance with coffee. I describe some of the scandals surrounding coffee, such as the petition by the women of London to ban coffee and how an illicit affair resulted in the largest coffee industry in the world. I recount coffee's role in the arts, exemplified by the Bach Coffee Cantata, a café that launched Picasso's career, and a TV drama in South Korea that threw the entire country into a coffee craze. Closer to home, I look at the role of coffee at high-tech companies and the activities surrounding coffee on the Web today.

Karina Halevy welcoming beans from "*the cool Andy Sprenger*" of Ceremony Coffee in Annapolis, Maryland.

This is also a story of my personal journey of discovery, one that was aided by today's indispensable tools such as Google, Facebook and Twitter. My worldwide network of computer science colleagues has been an incredible resource, leading me into the world of coffee experts, insiders, and connoisseurs. This journey has been a transformation from searching for coffee stories to stories being funneled to me. As I cruise around Google headquarters, I am now accustomed to being stopped by colleagues who eagerly clue me in on yet another coffee-related factoid.

When I started this project, I had no idea how expansive its scope would become, how enriching the adventure would turn out to be, or how profound an impact it would have on my family. Halfway into the project, my wife Oriana, a devout worshipper of fine teas, started appreciating gourmet coffee and craving her macchiatone every morning. Fortunately, around the same time, our four year-old son Kasper developed a fascination with the process of making espresso drinks. He now insists on hands-on participation in our macchiatone, macchiato and espresso rituals. Our daughter Karina has become enamored with the performing aspect of barista competitions. It is gratifying to have my family share my keen interest in the entire "seed to cup" journey of the humble coffee bean. Finally, and perhaps most profoundly, this project has instilled in me a new identity: I now feel very comfortable introducing myself as a coffee culturalist and author rather than a computer scientist.

Alon Halevy
Los Altos, California
Autumn, 2011

THE WORLD OF COFFEE

When I started exploring the world of coffee, I expected to find a relatively mature industry with well-understood practices. However, I was shocked to find a dynamic collection of passionate professionals who seem to advance the state of the art every time they pull a shot of espresso. This section provides the backdrop for a tour of the world of coffee by highlighting events and issues that both pervade in and act as focal points for the industry. These activities are rapidly fostering a progressive community that connects all parts of the coffee ecosystem and enabling farmers, roasters, and baristas from all over the world to seek collaboration, encourage innovation, and pursue excellence with the ultimate goal of elevating coffee to the status of a noble beverage.

We begin by examining the competitive flare of the coffee world. Every year since 2000, an ambassador of the coffee world is crowned at the World Barista Championship (WBC), the pinnacle of coffee competitions. Much more than about judging, winning and launching exciting career opportunities for the winning baristas, this annual event has become an entertaining venue for gathering, learning, displaying new techniques and spreading coffee knowledge to a wider audience. Over the years, the competition has shifted from emphasizing the technical aspects of coffee preparation to providing deeper knowledge of the coffee beans and complementary processing and extracting methods that accentuate the full expression of sublime flavors.

The Cup of Excellence is a farmer-centric competition that began in Brazil in 1999 and has since expanded to eight other coffee producing countries. Farmers compete by submitting samples of their best lots to be judged by an international jury of cuppers. While the winners have their moments of glory, the broader goal is to promote excellence in farming communities and to help foster direct relationships between farmers and specialty coffee buyers. In contrast to the traditional practice of buying nameless bins that include coffee from hundreds of farmers, specialty coffee buyers work directly with individual farmers and compensate them for their efforts.

We turn next to answering the question: what issues preoccupy coffee professionals these days that pervade many of their "geeking out" discussions at coffee-related competitions, conferences, and training workshops? These range from general and technical trends in coffee growing, roasting, and brewing, to complex and multidimensional issues such as sustainability.

Last but certainly not least, we visit the author's home base, Google headquarters in Mountain View, California. Google's avant-garde coffee culture is on the bleeding edge among technology company peers. Its compelling environment inspired my global coffee quest and concomitant coffee book project.

*"The 21st century will determine
whether coffee joins wine and tea
as a noble beverage."*

—GEORGE HOWELL,
pioneer of specialty coffee in the United States

COFFEE: A Competitive Sport

ON JUNE 23, 2011, I ROAMED THROUGH THE OLYMPIA CON-VENTION CENTER IN LONDON like a child in a candy store. It was the first day of the European Specialty Coffee Association's annual meeting and the hall was abuzz with vendors displaying coffee-related wares galore. I was offered not only complimentary espresso drinks of my choice, but also sumptuous cookies, muffins, chocolates and croissants, along with an array of exotic smoothies to wash them all down. I must have gained at least five pounds just traversing the exhibit hall.

Barista setups during competition are meticulously arranged.

I finally made it to the entrance to the World Barista Championship ("WBC") competition area, which was behind yet another free espresso bar that was serving award-winning beans and a brew bar that was displaying the latest and greatest manual brewing devices. On the center stage stood three café-style barista stations. A competitor was concocting a slick presentation at one station with multiple cameras hovering over him at a slight distance, while another competitor was setting up shop in the adjacent station. The scene was spasmodically interrupted by the emcee (typically a top performer at this venue in previous years) stirring up the crowd of several hundred very caffeinated spectators with calls like *"Let's have it for the first set of cappuccinos!"* and the exuberant applause that followed. Several hundred coffee enthusiasts were following the competition and discussing every detail online in a chat room.

The WBC is the pinnacle of events in the barista world. The fifty or so national champions who compete in this three-day event need to first jump through several qualifying hoops in their home countries. Each barista spends months, sometimes even years, training for a moment of glory in the international spotlight. The training often entails tasting dozens of coffees to ascertain the consummate beans, roasting and re-roasting the beans to release their most alluring expression, and perfecting a 15-minute presentation where every move is choreographed and every utterance carefully planned in advance. As the world's coffee ambassador for one year, the winner will travel extensively, give presentations, train baristas and judges, pull espresso shots, and help promote specialty coffee through active engagement with the media.

Mike Phillips pouring his signature drink, demonstrating the different tastes of naturals, honey-processed and washed coffee.

So what do the baristas actually do at this grand competition? Each barista puts on a 15-minute show that is performed to the backdrop of his or her musical choice, and sometimes with an item of distinctive clothing to accentuate personal flair. The competitor's goal is to impress four sensory judges, two technical judges, and one head judge, each of whom fills out a very detailed score sheet while watching closely. The barista usually begins with a short narrative about the origin of the coffee beans and highlights the different flavors the judges should be looking out for (e.g., maple, chocolate, blueberry). Then, in a skillfully orchestrated sequence of moves, the barista proceeds to prepare four quintessential espressos, followed by four cappuccinos each of which is effortlessly adorned with impressive latte art. While the barista performs, the technical judges provide an entertaining side show as they jostle for position to inspect the consistency of the barista's dosing, efficient use of coffee and milk, and the cleanliness of the station.

The theatrics reach a climax with the preparation of "signature" drinks, where baristas have the opportunity to use the extra paraphernalia and ingredients that they have laboriously transported to the competition site to showcase their creative savvy. These luscious drinks are supposed to be "coffee forward," meaning the tastes of coffee, whether bold, subtle, or nuanced, must be accentuated rather than overpowered by flavorings (in contrast to, say, a Starbucks skinny cinnamon dolce latte). To limit the range of possible combinations, alcohol is not allowed as flavoring in these signature drinks. Those who enjoy the pleasure of alcoholic coffee drinks may rise to the challenges of a separate competition entitled "World Coffee in Good Spirits."

The WBC has been held since 2000, when 12 national champions gathered in Monte Carlo for the inaugural competition. The competition's format, the brainchild of Norwegian economist and coffee specialist Alf Kramer, was first tested for two years in Norway before going global. Incidentally, the first world champion was Robert Thoresen, a Norwegian. In the earlier years of the championship, the Scandinavians dominated the competition with four world champions from Denmark and two from Norway.

Over the years, the competition has shifted from emphasizing the technical aspects of coffee preparation to providing deeper knowledge of the coffee beans, processing, and preparation. In London, the two-time Barista Champion of the United States Mike Phillips gave a textbook performance that demonstrated the combined knowledge of coffee processing and barista skills.

Mike showcased three coffees from Coope Dota, a cooperative in Costa Rica. He illustrated how the choice of processing method at harvest gives rise to different taste profiles of the beans. These differences were expertly exhibited in his tripartite signature drink. The first component, which he referred to as the palette cleanser, underscored the cleanliness, clarity and tart cherry flavor of the washed coffee (processed by removing the pulp and the mucilage before drying the bean in its husk). He poured a shot of espresso (after skimming off the crema to reduce the bitterness) into a glass with sparkling mineral water and a little bit of tart cherry juice. The second part of the signature drink sought to highlight the sweet and full-bodied characteristics of honey-processed coffee (where the bean is dried with the pulp and the mucilage, allowing more of the sweetness to seep into the bean). Mike poured a nectarous and savory date reduction with Moscovado sugar into the espresso shot. He instructed the judges to give the drink a swirl before taking a first sip that gave them mostly the espresso flavor. He then asked them to drink the rest, at which point the flavor of the date reduction had kicked in. Finally, the

The most common espresso-based drinks found around the world. Local preferences vary in the amounts of milk foam and steamed milk.

last part of the drink aimed to convey the spicy sweetness and fruity nature of fully natural-processed coffee (where the cherry is dried in the skin). The addition of ginger rhubarb reduction and agave to the espresso shot resulted in a piquant drink with a kiss of gingerbread zest.

At this point you are probably convinced that your life calling is to be a judge in these competitions. Before you quit your day job, read on just a little more. Roukiat Delrue, one of only a handful of people in the world who is certified to be a head judge of the WBC, clued me in on the prerequisites for judging which entail quite a bit more than sheer motivation to imbibe the sublime signature drinks. To be considered as a WBC judge, one first needs to be experienced at judging national competitions. That kind of certification requires at least a two-day workshop where attendees learn the myriad rules and go through mock competitions. Those who accumulate two years of national judging experience become eligible to apply for attendance at a WBC judge training workshop. Those with a passing scores of 80% or higher on tests administered through the training workshops will earn the coveted WBC judging certificates. As a final test of their true resolve, invitees to judge at the WBC are required to pay their own expenses and to attend a two-day calibration workshop prior to the competition.

The sensory judges listening attentively to a barista's presentation.

As detailed by a fascinating 33-page document, the scoring of the performances is quite intricate. In a nutshell and among many other criteria, the espresso will be judged on the quality of the crema and the balance of its taste. The cappuccino will be evaluated for its visual appearance (whether it is latte art or traditional), consistency, perfect serving temperature, persistence of the foam, and *"a harmonious balance of rich sweet milk/espresso."* For the signature beverage, the judges will consider the craft of storytelling and the fit between the story and the beans being used, finesse of presentation, originality of creation and, of course, taste. In all of

The technical judges inspect the competitor's every move.

these, the taste categories weigh higher in the final scoring. The rules even specify that the judges need to follow "reasonable" instructions from the barista. For example, if the barista requests that the judges drink the entire cup, they must follow. If no instructions are provided, the judges are obliged to take at least two sips.

The WBC is about much more than winning, judging, and launching new career opportunities for the winners. At its core, the competition is about bringing the coffee ecosystem together and creating camaraderie among countries and continents, and among baristas,

Alejandro Mendez of El Salvador raises his 2011 First Place trophy.

Anette Moldvaer of Square Mile Coffee holds up the winning cup at the 2007 World Cup Tasters Championship.

roasters and farmers. Behind the scenes, baristas often help each other in their own preparations and even train together months in advance. On the performance floor, fans often sport uniform T-shirts with their national colors to support their champ.

Returning to the June 2010 WBC, 12 semifinalists emerged after two days of first round performance. From them, the representatives of Australia, Denmark, Greece, Guatemala, Ireland, and the United States were selected as finalists. Like many of the other competitors in London, these finalists were all competing for the second or even third time at the WBC. The crowd huddled in animated excitement and palpable anticipation as Gwilym Davies, the 2009 World Barista Champion, called out the final rankings. The frenzy peaked when only two competitors were left standing, Mike Phillips of the United States and Raul Rodas of Guatemala, both from a continent that had never won the championship. When Raul's name was called at #2, the two exchanged a poignantly emotional hug. Raul was the first competitor from a coffee growing country to even make it to the finals. His outstanding placement at the 2010 WBC has made him an inspirational hero to baristas throughout the world. Mike Phillips, who started his coffee career merely four years earlier as a bag packer in a Chicago warehouse, made history that day by becoming the first American to win the world title.

A year later at the 2011 WBC held in Bogotá Colombia, a very similar scenario unfolded. The last two competitors left standing were the champion of the United States Pete Licata and the champion of El Salvador, Alejandro Mendez. But this time the order was flipped: Alejandro became the first competitor from a producing country to take the World Barista Champion title. The momentous nature and tremendous excitement of his win continue to reverberate throughout the coffee world.

Competing on Other Coffee Skills

Several other coffee-related competitions are held annually and highlight various talents and cultures. Although the rules of these competitions are often moving targets, their spirit remains the same from one year to the next. Of course, in addition to the glory that comes with succeeding in these competitions, a commonly heard and oft-repeated motivation is that baristas enter the competitions to improve their skills and learn new ones. And indeed, all the months of effort culminate in those outcomes. The winner is simply the one who performed the best on the competition day.

CUP TASTING: Held since 2004, the "World Cup Tasters Championship" is a sophisticated test for the palate. Instead of judging or identifying coffees, the competition focuses on discriminating coffees. Each competitor completes eight "triangulation" tests. In each test, the competitor is given three cups of coffee, two of which are identical. The competitors need to decide which of the cups contains the different one. The winner at each stage is the competitor who manages to guess correctly most often. In the event of a tie, speed will determine the winner. The tests become progressively challenging toward the later stages of the competition. Unlike the other competitions that require deliberations among the judges, the results here are tallied in real time in what often makes a pretty intense and dramatic show. After the competitor decides which coffee is different in each triangle, the other cups are removed. The competitor then lifts each of the remaining eight cups one by one so the crowd can see the bottom of the cup. A red dot under the cup signifies a correct answer that gets the competitor another point.

Viktoriya Vlasenko from the Ukraine at the 2011 World in Good Spirits competition in Maastricht.

COFFEE IN GOOD SPIRITS: The "World Coffee in Good Spirits" competition combines the skills of a barista with those of a bartender. The competitors create two traditional Irish coffees from the requisites of coffee, whiskey and cream. The Irish coffees must exhibit a sublime combination of the three ingredients and have the cream nicely separated from the rest of the drink. In the second half of the show, the competitor creates a signature drink that exhibits their creative panache. Competitors at the 2011 competition produced several drinks with orange-colored toppings because they were asked to concoct a drink that pays homage to the host country, the Netherlands. An interesting twist to this competition arose from the rule permitting the use of "any legal ingredient." Because drugs such as marijuana are "legal" in the Netherlands, the competition applied the narrower and more broadly accepted definition of "legal substances" to exclude drugs.

LATTE ART: The "World Latte Art Championship" is where baristas, or should I say, artists, compete on the beauty and intricacy of the patterns they design by combining milk and coffee. They compose three drinks: a macchiato, a latte and a signature drink. In the signature drink they are allowed to use additional tools to make their designs more intricate. To ensure no coincidences, the competitors are required to share their designs with the judges ahead of time and to produce two identical drinks with that design. Competitors are scored on the originality, complexity, contrast and creativity of their designs. This competition is a pure feast for the eyes.

Lavishly clad Jin-Seol Bae from Korea creates an elaborate table setting for the judges on the way to winning the 2011 Czeve/Ibrik Championship.

CEZVE/IBRIK: Inaugurated in 2009, the *Cezve/Ibrik* competition celebrates the culture of coffee preparation that is prevalent in the Middle East, North Africa and Eastern Europe. The *cezve* (known also as *ibrik*) is a pot with the long handle that is made especially for preparing and serving coffee. The competitors first prepare the basic Turkish coffee for the two judges, and then create a second beverage in which they may add sweeteners and spices. Finally, they create a signature drink showcasing their creativity. The competitors' elaborate costumes and complex table settings provide entertaining

Gianni Cassatini, together with M'lissa Owens, a barista from Intelligentsia Coffee, cheering the competitors.

A peacock created by the Australian latte art champion, Kirby Berlin.

side shows in this competition. The judges join in on the fun by wearing traditional garb as they sip the lovely drinks.

BREWERS CUP: The Brewers Cup was introduced in 2011 in response to the rising excitement for hand-brewing techniques such as filter pour-over, the syphon, and the aeropress. In the first round, all the competitors are given the same coffee beans and may use any technique they desire to brew and impress the judges. In the second round, the competitors bring their own beans and go into elaborate explanations about their coffee and the preparation method as they brew the coffee for the judges. As stated in the official rules and regulations of the Brewers Cup, the judges are looking for a champion who *"prepares brewed coffee beverages of exemplary quality, delivers outstanding customer service, can articulate the taste experience provided by their brewed coffee beverages, and delivers an exceptional overall coffee service experience."*

The Baristas' Godfather

No discussion of barista competitions would be complete without mentioning Gianni Cassatini, the baristas' Cheerleader-in-Chief. Whether you are a World Barista Champion, an aspiring young barista, or a coffee book author, you are guaranteed a royal and effusive greeting from Gianni Cassatini, the public relations consultant to high-end espresso machine manufacturer Nuova Simonelli. After working for Johnson Controls for three decades, 74 year-old Sicily-born Gianni could easily be sitting at his Vancouver home and leading a quiet retirement life. However, his lifelong passion for coffee led him to answer a call from the CEO of Nuova Simonelli, a fellow Italian émigré who had settled in Vancouver. Since Nuova Simonelli became an espresso machine sponsor at the WBC in 2009, Gianni has attended every barista competition he can, at the regional, national and international levels.

It is a small wonder that Gianni has become one of the most beloved figures in the specialty-coffee industry. This omnipresent patriarch of baristas is one hell of an Italian character. Even though his official role at the competitions is to provide technical support for the machines, his infectious enthusiasm and endearing gregariousness prompt him to talk shop with everyone. He thrives on helping baristas behind the scenes, cheering them on stage, and most importantly, taking an honest interest in each and every one of them. When he met the parents of Mike Phillips, he introduced himself as Mike's "second father." That title has stuck in the barista world. When a bunch of rambunctious baristas were having some late night fun at Camp Pull-a-Shot in 2010, Gianni did not hesitate to join the action when he was called to do a keg stand by the cheering crowd. As a sign of his true celebrity, there is an official Gianni collector's item, a T-shirt that bears his image on the front. ✒

CUP OF EXCELLENCE: The Oscars of Coffee

ON NOVEMBER 19, 2010, THE CROWD OF 300 IN A PACKED HOTEL AUDITORIUM in the Brazilian city of Poços de Caldas erupted in wild applause as the name of the winning coffee farm was announced at the award ceremony of the 11th Brazil Cup of Excellence Competition (CoE). Cláudio Carneiro Pinto, the owner of Grota São Pedro, an organic farm in Minas Gerais, was now being showered with admiration typically reserved in this country for goal-scoring soccer heroes.

In practical terms, winning the competition meant that Cláudio could sell his coffee for over $25 per pound, more than 10 times as much as the C-price, the typical price per pound of coffee fetched on the market at the same time.

Eduardo Ambrocio, the head judge, standing in the middle. On the right, Grant Rattray giving last minute instructions to the judges.

The market pricing was determined in an Internet auction that took place a couple of months following the competition, in which all the coffees that the international jury scored 84 points (the magic score that qualifies a coffee as "cup of excellence" grade) and above were eligible to participate. Aside from increasing his annual income, the win elevates Cláudio and his farm to a special status in the Brazilian coffee industry, the world's largest with over 350,000 farms. Grant Rattray, the managing director of the Alliance for Coffee Excellence (ACE–the organization that runs the competitions), mentioned that about half of the coffees from these auctions are typically bought by Japanese importers, about 15% by Americans, and the rest by Europeans and others. He explained the high Japanese share by the fact that Japanese roasters are better able to sell the coffees for higher prices in their markets because their clientele is more willing to pay more for quality coffee.

An intense week of coffee cupping and animated discussions led up to the award ceremony. The international jury, consisting mostly of coffee buyers, roasters and café owners, assembled at the facilities of the Brazilian Specialty Coffee Association near the city of Machado. Led by head judge Eduardo Ambrocio from Guatemala, the jurors spent four days going through three rounds of competition. They started with high standards—all the coffees they cupped had already received a score of 84 or above from a national Brazilian cupping jury that met the week before and selected 47 coffees from the 250 that were submitted to the competition.

During each of these cupping sessions, the jurors gathered in a room wearing their black apron uniforms and carrying their main weapon, the cupping spoon. To ensure that only the coffees' aroma came into play, a sign at the entrance to the cupping room explicitly prohibited perfumes. Each cupping table was neatly arranged with rows of coffee samples labeled 1 to 8. For each sample there were four cups of ground beans, one for every juror. As always, the cuppings were done on a completely blind basis—jurors knew nothing about the coffees, certainly not the originating farms.

The cupping sessions began with aroma evaluation. Initially, each juror smelled the dry ground coffee, and then smelled again when water filled the cups. Four minutes later, the cuppers smelled the coffees yet again as they 'broke the crust,' at which point additional bouquets of fragrance explode from the cup.

At that point, the room turned into a rhapsody of whizzing and slurping sounds as the jurors inhaled the coffee on their cupping spoons, all the while attempting to spread the coffee evenly over their tongues as expertly as possible. As they moved among coffees, they dipped their spoons in cups of hot water to avoid cross-contamination. They scored each coffee on their cupping form for cleanliness, sweetness, acidity, flavor, balance, mouthfeel and aftertaste. The cupping went on for 45 minutes, enabling the cuppers to also evaluate the characteristics of the coffees as they cooled down. Every juror assigned each coffee a composite score between 0 and 100 that was immediately fed into a database by the support staff who then tallied the points.

The debrief session that followed gave the judges an opportunity to share a few snacks to refresh their palates. This is where the judges' creative juices flowed forth and colorful coffee characterizations rolled off their gleeful tongues. After comparing their scoring notes, the jurors discussed the attributes detected and the flavors sensed in each coffee sample. A kaleidoscopic array of flavors were mentioned, from common ones such as chocolate, sugar cane, caramel, floral tones, almonds, red berries, blueberries, grape, and mango, to less expected ones such as peapods, raisins, rhubarb, and even green pepper. The wired jurors articulated their own impressions without reservation. There were no right or wrong answers. Some comments were even more vividly expressive, such as tasting *"pineapple with ham," "herbatious," "molly sweet,"* or an effusively back-handed compliment, *"Wow, this coffee was so good, it could be an Ethiopian."* Andrew Hetzel, the owner of Café Makers in Kona, Hawaii, took the prize for the most memorable description: *"Yay, I just got new tires!"* He

Colleen Anunu of Gimme! Coffee inhaling the aromatics.

insisted that was a compliment to one of the coffees he had cupped.

A novice in the room may have been able to follow the discussions up until this point, but all bets were off when the jurors start expounding the coffee's acidity. Acidity gives coffee its spark and is the primary basis for evaluating coffee. Apparently, acidity can be citric, elegant, refined, juicy, balanced, round, bright, well-structured, refreshing, brilliant, sparkling, or any combination of the above.

After the first two days, the jury narrowed the field of competitors down to 36 coffees from the initial 47 entrants. To make it to the second round, the coffees had to garner an average score of 84 or above. These coffees were cupped again in the second round to determine which would make it to the top ten.

On the last day, the jurors arrived with great enthusiasm and anticipation, eager for the dream session of cupping the top ten coffees of Brazil side by side. If on most days the jurors typically spit out the coffee after tasting, today they often swallowed each sample with pleasure. After an intense thirty minutes, the jury adjourned to discuss the coffees and erupted in group applause as the winning coffee emerged.

Between sessions, Silvio Leite, one of the pioneers of specialty coffee in Brazil and a co-founder of the CoE, took time to explain the genesis of the competition. In a nutshell, the competition grew out of frustration at the lack of excitement for Brazilian coffees among specialty coffee buyers. In the 1990's, the United Nations and the International Coffee Organization (ICO) funded the Gourmet Project in an attempt to help five countries (Brazil, Burundi, Ethiopia, Papua New Guinea and Uganda) improve the pricing they were receiving for their coffees. As part of this project, the triumvirate of Silvio, Marcelo Viera, head of the Brazilian Specialty Coffee Association at the time, and American coffee icon George Howell worked with ten farms in Brazil to improve the quality of their beans. As Silvio lamented, even after significant improvements in quality, Brazilian coffees were still considered the *"best team of the second division."*

As the Gourmet Project drew to a close, the triumvirate, together with Susie Spindler, the marketing director for the project and an image-branding expert, and Don Holly from the Specialty Coffee Association of America began searching in earnest for creative solutions to this challenge. The idea of creating a quality competition with an international jury bubbled up. However, they did not think that would suffice. As Susie puts it, *"You cannot take a winning certificate to the bank."* In those early days of commerce on the Internet, they were inspired by the success of Ebay to create an auction for the winning coffees, with the aim of garnering higher prices and generating excitement. An auction would also enable easy and inclusive access to roasters who could bid on the coffees.

They went ahead with the idea when the ICO came up with the initial funding, notwithstanding skepticism from many quarters including the Brazilian farmers themselves. George Howell ensured that the new cupping form he designed enabled the cuppers to express a wide range of coffee attributes. In the first competition held in 1999, 310 farmers submitted samples and the jury included 14 cuppers. In the first auction, coffees were sold for $2.90 per pound, compared to the 70-80 cents they were fetching on the market. The second competition was held in 2000 with a much bigger jury whose members at one point were so impressed with the coffees that they asked: *"What country are we in?"* All of a sudden, Brazilian coffees had come of age and their extraordinary quality was being recognized. The 2010 competition was the eleventh one in Brazil. As both a symbol and celebration of its continuity, the co-founder's daughter and expert cupper Jenny Howell served as a member of the international jury.

The impact of the Cup of Excellence has been far-reaching on multiple levels.

The international jury votes on coffees' scores.

Cláudio Carneiro Pinto receiving First Place in the Cup of Excellence of Brazil, 2010

Geographically, the competition has expanded to Bolivia, Costa Rica, Honduras, Guatemala, Rwanda, Nicaragua, Colombia and El Salvador and a total of 60 competitions have been held so far. Panama has followed the same model, but administers the competitions itself. For the producing countries, the program has helped set standards for coffee cupping and evaluation. Heart-warming stories about how the winning growers have used the proceeds of the auctions, whether they paid down debt, invested in better farming techniques, serviced and maintained their equipment, or sent their children to school, abound. For coffee buyers and the industry, the program forged a direct link between farmers and importers, thus paving the way to direct trade in the coffee industry. When you enjoy a cup of coffee from Brazil, it is no longer simply a Brazilian. You can find out exactly which farm it came from and when it was harvested. Recognition of the coffee farms is following in the footsteps of vineyards, a long overdue acknowledgement and stamp of approval. ☞

COFFEE TRENDS AND CONTROVERSIES

TO A NEWCOMER, THE MOST STRIKING ASPECTS OF THE COFFEE WORLD are the passion and dedication of its professionals, how quickly the industry is changing, and the numerous hotly debated issues. After all, coffee has been around for hundreds of years, and one would expect that it has all been figured out. There is a plethora of blogs from passionate baristas, roasters and coffee buyers and sites for coffee-related discussions on the Web. One can easily spend hours a day following the community's tweeters. For coffee-related comic relief, sprudge.com regularly offers off-the-wall stories. Led by *Barista Magazine* and *Roast Magazine*, a number of periodicals help deepen coffee and industry knowledge. Coffee professionals are constantly traveling around the world to competitions, coffee farms, conferences and training camps. The hard-core ones even pack their own aeropresses, hand grinders and coffee beans hand in hand with their passports, just in case they end up in a coffee-challenged location. They gather in small groups for what they refer to as "geeking out" sessions where they thrash out the nitty gritty details of coffee growing, roasting, brewing and the latest machinery and artistry.

To set the context and introduce an important term used in the industry, the folks we discuss here all belong to the *third wave* of coffee. The term has been used in many ways since it was introduced by Trish Rothgeb from San Jose, California who had taken her roasting expertise to Oslo, Norway where she worked with the first World Barista Champion Robert Thoresen and introduced Oslo to lighter roasts. When asked to explain the term, Trish quotes her partner and co-owner of Wrecking Ball Coffee, Nick Cho: *"The first wave is all about consumption. The second wave is about enjoyment and defining specialty. The third wave allows the coffee to speak for itself. It's all about appreciating each coffee for what it truly is and takes whatever necessary steps to highlight the amazing unique character in every coffee."* In practical terms, the first wave can be classified as anything that preceded Peet's and Starbucks, and the third wave are the folks who obsessively explore single origin coffees, innovate on every aspect of coffee preparation, and invest in creating direct and lasting relationships with coffee farmers. In even more pragmatic terms (and admitting author bias), once you have experienced coffee from these third wave folks, there is simply no turning back.

So what issues are on the minds of these coffee geeks? The following will give you a taste for the buzz.

The Wine Comparison

The general lack of widespread appreciation for good coffee is a critical issue facing the coffee industry because it affects all levels of the trade, from the growers to the roasters and baristas. At fine dining establishments, patrons are handed lengthy wine menus with prices ranging from the affordable to the astronomical. Anticlimactic offerings of mediocre to poor quality coffees at the end of these gourmet meals could really put a damper on the entire dining experience. For the baristas the situation is even more demeaning: to open a bottle of wine the waiter staff only needs a corkscrew because the hard work was done at the winery; for coffee, significant artistry and skill are needed

The drip bar at Mocca Espressobar in Oslo, Norway includes the aeropress, chemex, syphon and hario drip.

at serving time to ensure a quality cup. With rather narrow operating profit margins, restaurants save money by offering low quality coffee. As far as the specialty coffee folks are concerned, there are multiple reasons why this is an unacceptable state of affairs. First, wouldn't patrons of fine restaurants expect a great cup of coffee to cap off an expensive meal? Second, why not develop a culture where coffee quality is prized over quantity and customers are willing to pay more for a better cup? In New York, the classy restaurant Eleven Madison Park recently rethought their coffee strategy and now offers patrons a table-side coffee service where they may view the barista's skillful and meticulous coffee preparation using a syphon or a Chemex. If consumers spend more money for higher quality coffees, baristas can get better training, roasters can apply their artistry more widely, and coffee importers can seek higher quality beans and compensate the farmers for their additional efforts. Unlike wine, which is viewed as a semi-luxury good that is usually consumed with dinner (in countries like France, lunch), coffee is viewed as a necessity to wake up and stay alert throughout the day. Some even believe that it is a basic human right to have access to coffee! Since coffee is traded as a commodity, the price of coffee fluctuates depending on the speculation of traders sitting in high rises in New York who may well have no idea about the vast differences in coffee quality.

To be fair, this indifferent attitude is not ubiquitous. For example, there is far greater appreciation for higher quality coffees in countries such as Japan and Norway. Because consumers there are willing to shell out more money for a premium cup, the base line for coffee quality in these countries is higher than anywhere else and many of the Cup of Excellence coffees end up being consumed there. In some high-end cafés, prices differ markedly depending on the quality of the coffee (as opposed to the amount of milk or flavoring requested).

Even though it will take more time for specialty coffees to achieve the same status as premium wines, the movers and shakers of the coffee industry are constantly working to educate their clientele about high quality coffee through cuppings, lectures, and competitions. Fortunately, it is extremely difficult to go back to the mundane and lifeless commercial coffees after experiencing the sheer pleasure of a cup of specialty coffee. ✎

Freshness, Seasonality and Transparency

Leading coffee buyers and roasters in the world go to great lengths to ensure freshness, seasonality, and transparency of their coffees. Freshness is a fundamental coffee quality metric. In a supermarket, the coffee isle may be right next to the cereal isle and the packaging of the products may look similar in many ways. However, as the founder of Intelligentsia Doug Zell puts it, coffee *"is not like a box of cereal."* Rather, it is a perishable agricultural product whose quality deteriorates with time just like fruits and vegetables. Serving fresh coffee is the basic hallmark of a good café.

The concept of seasonality takes the idea of freshness even further by emphasizing the most recently harvested coffee that a particular season affords. It is a tricky quality metric because it often conflicts with a vendor's desire for consistency (serving customers a consistent flavor year round).

Transparency is another metric that is high on the minds of coffee professionals. Most coffees sold in the world come from large bins

> Coffee bags now include origin, roast date and other details.

into which farmers of a particular region deposit their coffee. Transparency refers to the idea of specifying which farm(s) a particular coffee comes from and in some cases, even the micro-lot within the farm. Transparency also encompasses the idea of providing consumers information about the exact method used to process the coffee, the altitude on which it was grown, and the specific environmental practices used on the particular farm. Transparency is therefore a mechanism of rewarding individual farmers for their efforts and investments.

Leading coffee buyers engage in significant effort to raise awareness of these values in the eyes of consumers. They start with their coffee labels that specify the farm the beans came from, dates of harvest and roasting and in some cases, the date on which the coffee will peak for consumption.

Because coffee loses quality at all stages of processing, there is an ongoing quest for more knowledge within the industry about how to preserve the quality of coffee after harvesting. Given appropriate conditions, green coffee can be stored for longer periods without losing quality and offers several benefits including the abilities to create the same blends year after year and to mitigate against seasonal supply crises. However, the questions of which coffees can be stored longer and why remain largely a mystery. Upon roasting, coffee typically reaches its peak flavor after two to fourteen days and then starts its flavor profile's downward spiral. The Illy Coffee Company is well-known for investing vast research resources into vacuum packaging methods that enable the coffee to be shipped anywhere across the world, sit for months on the shelf, and still offer a consistent taste. Coffee flavor starts to weaken immediately after grinding. It is therefore crucial to grind just prior to brewing.

To start understanding these issues and assess the tradeoffs, the Global Coffee Quality Research Initiative (GCQRI) launched in October 2010 with a meeting that brought together a wide array of experts from the coffee industry. The goal of GCQRI is to fund research into fundamental questions regarding coffee quality and share the results with the wider community and with consumers.

Two methods for processing coffee at one mill in El Salvador. The darker beans are being dried in the cherry using the naturals method. The lighter ones had been depulped and washed before drying.

The Comeback of Drip Coffee

Hanging out with the coffee geeks could easily lead one to conclude that to be a true connoisseur of coffee you need to love drip coffee (broadly referring to any coffee that is not espresso). But do not let your mind wander to the image of the percolator that adorns office kitchens worldwide and only gets refilled when its contents become completely undrinkable. We are talking about a new family of brewing techniques where coffee is prepared one cup at a time, according to your express preferences and of course, with the highest quality beans. The most common method is the pour-over bar where water is slowly poured over the coffee grounds in skillful fashion, using a Hario or a Chemex. It can be the more theatrical syphon preparation, or an aeropress, the convenient travel companion for the diehard. Many specialty coffee shops have reconfigured their counter spaces to allow for the exhibition of these new brewing techniques. A growing number of competitors at barista competitions has started incorporating drip coffee into their performances. As mentioned earlier, the World Brewers Cup was inaugurated in 2011 to celebrate the artistry and technique that go into preparing drip coffee.

Why this turn of events? What has happened to the romance with espresso? Some say that because espresso was designed to extract coffee very quickly, it is fundamentally inferior to slower brewing techniques that bring out more flavors. Others note that espresso drinks typically need to be consumed relatively quickly, while slowly sipping drip coffee is much more conducive for leisurely conversations. Moreover, the unhurried pace of drinking allows for detecting the changing flavors of the coffee as it cools down.

Not all coffee enthusiasts are enchanted by drip coffee. Some argue that a second espresso is a much better way to prolong a conversation. Colin Harmon, the two-time barista champion of Ireland and finalist at the 2009 and 2010 World Barista Championships, laments the disenchantment with espresso on his blog. He suggests that the reason for drip coffee's comeback is that there is so much to improve compared to the standard practice in coffee shops. Copious information notwithstanding, he feels that there is still much to be learned about espresso preparation. Regardless of the debate, espresso and drip represent two different expressions of coffee and will ultimately continue to be celebrated side by side.

The Naturals Debate

Should coffee be dried in its cherry or should it first be washed off of its enclosing cherry? The former is called the naturals method, while the latter is called washed processing (and yes, there are several in between methods as well). Some in the coffee world are fanatical about naturals, while others oppose it with equal or even greater passion.

The naturals debate is not new, but gets reignited on occasion. Geoff Watts, the Director of Coffee at Intelligentsia Coffee in Chicago and their main coffee buyer, recently indicated in his decadal prediction of coffee trends that he hoped the *"near fanatical obsession"* with naturals process-

Syphon

Pour-Over

ing will become a *"footnote in the history of coffee."* Watts claims that the naturals method presents additional risks to the farmer because of higher incidences of defects and loss of nuance in the resulting cup. Most agree with the first half of this argument because when the coffees are wash processed, it is easier to find defective and unripe cherries whose presence can significantly degrade the quality of the cup. The crux of the argument centers around taste. The 2007 World Barista Champion and blogger extraordinaire James Hoffmann counters Watts by claiming that naturals not only have their distinctive flavors, but also enable retaining the full range of coffee flavors much better than washed processing.

Kopi Luwak

In keeping with its relentless effort to promote quality, the specialty coffee industry is also trying to repudiate the fanciful claims of "gimmick" coffees such as the *Kopi Luwak* that often carries a price tag of more than $50 per cup. The most frequent question I was asked while writing this book was: have you tried the coffee from the dung of the cat? The few who have actually splurged and tasted the coffee engage in lively debates about whether its taste is worth the steep price.

The fuss concerns the Asian Civet cat (*luwak*) whose natural habitats are found in parts of Indonesia and the Philippines. The civet has the unique olfactory ability to hone in on particularly ripe coffee cherries. The cat consumes the cherries (typically at night) and enjoys the pulp around the beans. The bean itself stays completely intact and ends up defecated after going though the digestive system. Farmers scour their fields looking for civet dung containing the beans. After thorough washings (hopefully!), the beans are roasted relatively lightly to produce a very unique flavor.

This supposed delicacy even got the attention of researchers from the University of Guelph in Canada who were curious about the chemical basis for the special flavors the coffee exhibits. In a 2004 article published in the journal *Food Research International*, the authors claim that the beans that go through the civet's digestive system come out harder, more brittle and darker than other beans. The explanation for the difference in taste is that the beans lose some of their protein during the digestive process and as a result produce a less bitter taste. Massimo Marcone, the researcher in charge of the study, describes the flavor as *"earthy, musty, syrupy, smooth and rich with jungle and chocolate undertones."*

Coffee Biology 101

Plantae → Embryophyta → Tracheophyta → Spermatophyta → Angiospermae → Tricolpate (Eudicots) → Core Tricolpate (Core Eudicots) → Asterids (Sympetales) → Core Asterids → Euasterids I → Gentianales → Rubiaceae → Coffea

Coffea has over 70 species, the two best-known of which are *C. arabica* and *C. canefora*. The species known as Robusta is a subspecies of *C. canefora*. Arabica and Robusta together account for over 98% of the world's coffee production (with Arabica accounting for about two thirds). To the best of our knowledge, the world is not missing out on any untapped delicacies by focusing on these two species.

Whereas Arabica has 44 chromosomes (2.2 billion base pairs) and is self-pollinating, Robusta is cross-pollinating and its genome is half the size of the Arabica. Robusta is more resistant to disease and typically produces more yield per hectare. Even though it contains about twice the amount of caffeine, its taste is considered far inferior to that of Arabica's. Of Arabica's over 150 varietals, Typica is the oldest and originated in the Kaffa region of Ethiopia. Other well known varietals such as Bourbon, Blue Mountain, Sumatra and Kona are either mutations or selections from Typica.

Esmeralda Special is a rare award-winning coffee that has set three online coffee auction records.

A civet cat held in a cage in downtown Seoul waiting to be fed coffee cherries.

Being a rather rare commodity, the coffee processed in this way commands very high prices on the market. Unfortunately, the "civet gold rush" has also spawned quite a few fake beans on the market, as well as farms where the cats are kept in cages and fed cherries rather than using their natural ability to forage the best ones.

On a trip to Indonesia, my parents in-law felt compelled to contribute to the research for this book and brought back a bag of Kopi Luwak. After tasting, I side strongly with the specialty industry folks on this one. However, as with any judgment relating to taste, the only way to find out is to try it yourself.

Sustainability

The demand for coffee, quality coffee in particular, is growing worldwide. Existing markets are expanding and potentially huge ones such as China and India are developing quickly. In parallel, climate change is affecting the viability of coffee production in some regions where coffee cultivation is an integral part of the social fabric. Changing climate patterns are forcing farmers to abandon certain farming regions or to move to higher altitudes where there is less farm area. Furthermore, in keeping with the global movement towards increased social responsibility, there is a collective desire to improve the economic conditions of the people growing and harvesting the cherries whose beans form the basis for our morning rituals. With all these factors at play, it comes as no surprise that the sustainability of coffee farming is foremost on the minds of many coffee professionals.

Sustainability is an incredibly complex issue. Contrary to widespread belief, sustainability encompasses much more than organic farming. True sustainability is based on balancing three pillars that are sometimes not completely aligned: economic, social and environmental. Adopting organic farming practices is just one illustration of this challenge. On the one hand, organic farming produces coffee that is healthier for the consumer due to a lower toxin content for the environment. This comes from a smaller carbon footprint, and shedding less toxins into the local rivers. On the other hand, a non-organic farm can produce substantially more coffee. Peter Giuliano, the current president of the Specialty Coffee Association of America and co-owner of Counter Culture Coffee, summarized with this analogy: "*Non-organic farming is like putting your farm on steroids. You can produce more in the short term but after a few years your yields may actually decrease.*" To make organic farming attractive to farmers, they need to be able to charge more money for their coffee.

Other examples of balancing the pillars of sustainability come from the failure of a few social programs in Central America. In Guatemala, seemingly impenetrable cultural barriers have prevented the successful implementation of the government's initiatives aimed at helping farmers from the indigenous population to adopt modern farming techniques that would improve their yields. El Salvador and other countries faced a different kind of problem when they launched land redistribution programs whose goal was to promote social equity in coffee farming: although the land recipients who had hitherto been slaves on larger farms were happy to be freed from slavery, they lacked the skills necessary to run their farms which were hardly sizable enough to pull them out of poverty. Sadly, the recent spike in coffee prices in 2011 has created yet another social problem around guarding farms from thefts and keeping farmers faithful to their co-ops when they receive better offers for their coffee from drive-by-night buyers.

To further complicate matters, reaping benefits from sustainable farming requires certification, such as Organic, Rainforest Alliance, or Fair Trade. Obtaining these certifications can be a long and expensive process that is out of reach for many farmers. Moreover, each of the certification methods has received its fair share of criticism for not promoting the true goal of sustainability. Fair Trade, which guarantees farmers a minimum price for their coffee that is above the market price, has been criticized for the fact that the price guarantees produce an artificial market mechanism that will ultimately hurt farmers rather than help them. In addition, Fair Trade certification is only available to cooperatives. The corruption that often seeps into cooperative management often prevents the higher prices paid for the coffee from trickling down to the farmers.

The increased attention to and resources spent on certification in the 1990's led to a controversy that still lingers in the coffee community today: Should the focus be on certification or on the quality of coffee? In some cases, the coffee buyers felt like they knew the farms' practices well enough to be able to "self-certify," though that practice dwindled after a

One of the many ways in which sustainability is pursued at Coope Dota in Costa Rica. The red "hill" of coffee cherry pulp is later processed to produce fertilizer with the help of worms.

Coffee cherry pulp

while. This controversy came to a head recently during the 2010 Good Food Awards (GFA) in San Francisco. The GFA prides itself on its commitment to food that is produced in a sustainable fashion. However, the language used in the competition rules was somewhat vague. When push came to shove, some of the coffees (Kenyan coffees in particular) that were chosen to be finalists based on their tastes were disqualified because they could not produce the certification required by the GFA.

Fortunately, the focus on quality often goes hand in hand with better sustainability practices. Farmers who are concerned with the overall environmental wellness of their farms are also those who are likely to pick only the ripest cherries and care for their trees. Re-

On the left, Allie Caran, a barista from Baltimore on her first visit to origin. In the middle, Peter Giuliano, co-owner of Counter Culture Coffee, a leading roasting company. On the right, Aida Batlle, a farmer from El Salvador who was also the first farmer to receive a barista certificate from the Bartisa Guild of America.

markable strides continue to be made worldwide in creating more sustainable coffee farms. Leading coffee buyers work closely with farmers to assist in the transition to organic farming and adjustment to new climate conditions. Consequently, there are more farms being transformed to organic, more effort placed on growing trees for shade, more water filtration projects, more widespread use of cherry pulp as fertilizer, and more programs for providing education and food to farm workers. Perhaps the most extreme example of striving for sustainability comes from Coope Dota, a farming cooperative in Costa Rica that we feature later in this book. They completed an unusual certification in April 2011: their entire operation, including the emissions produced during the transportation of their coffees, has achieved a neutral carbon footprint!

Sustainability is an issue that will continue to occupy the minds of coffee professionals for a long while. As Peter Giuliano cautions, while the coffee community has a good faith belief that it can solve the sustainability problem within its own microcosm, the reality is that the solutions must involve the multilateral powers and concerted efforts of governments, individuals and enterprises working toward the goal of balancing the needs of their people and the environment.

Communicating with customers

The topics above are only the tip of the iceberg. A common theme that pervades all the discussions among coffee professionals is how to communicate the issues to customers. Do customers even care? Are the coffee geeks ending up appearing elitist in their zeal to promote quality coffee? Even more fundamentally, is quality first and foremost on the minds of coffee drinkers or do they care more about the social interactions and ambiance of the coffee venue? Do memories of previous experiences evoked by coffee trump the importance of the quality of coffee? Does anyone have the right to tell me what good coffee is? Such a broad sociological survey is beyond the scope of this book. However, this book provides ample illustrations of how passionate coffee professionals are creating experiences that get their customers hooked on quality coffee. ✎

1. Brazil – 45,992

2. Vietnam – 16,000

3. Colombia – 10,500

4. Indonesia – 8,638

5. Ethiopia – 6,133

6. Mexico – 4,650

7. India – 4,372

8. Peru – 3,868

9. Honduras – 3,373

10. Guatemala – 3,370

11. Uganda – 3,300

12. Côte d'Ivoire – 2500

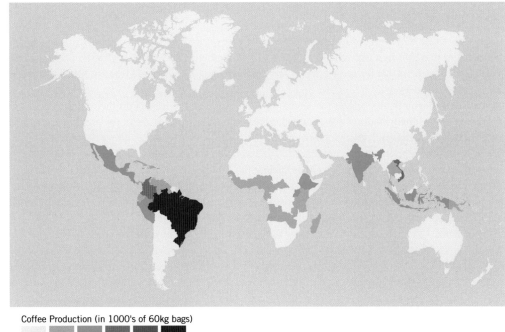

Coffee Production (in 1000's of 60kg bags)

0   45,992

Above: The coffee producing countries (as of 2010). Darker green indicates more production. The top producing countries are listed on the left (in 1000's of 60Kg bags). Below, the per capita coffee consumption in kg per year (as of 2008). Here darker brown indicates more consumption. The data is made available by the International Coffee Organization and World Research Institute.

1. Finland – 12

2. Solomon Islands – 11.8

3. Norway – 9.9

4. Namibia – 9

5. Denmark – 8.7

6. Netherlands – 8.4

7. Sweden – 8.2

8. Switzerland – 7.9

9. Bahrain – 6.8

10. Belgium – 6.8

11. Luxembourg – 6.8

12. Brunei – 6.6

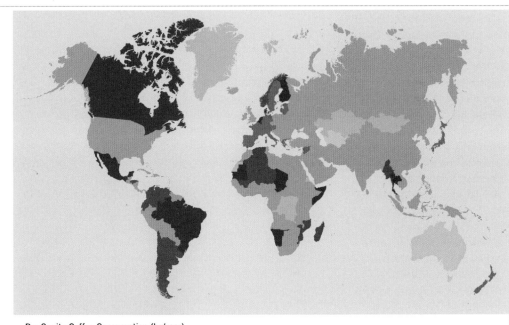

Per Capita Coffee Consumption (kg/year)

0   12

COFFEE GOOGLE STYLE

MUCH HAS BEEN WRITTEN ABOUT THE ENVIABLE PERKS ENJOYED BY SPOILED GOOGLERS, including three daily complimentary and excellent meals from a wide choice of gourmet and themed caféterias, subsidized on-campus massages, and 24/7 access to fully stocked micro kitchens that feature a dizzying array of fresh fruits, snacks and libations. Much less publicized is what an incredible place Google is for coffee lovers.

Many software companies realize that access to coffee has a direct impact on their bottom line. The business of writing computer programs requires many hours of concentrated mental effort that often peaks in the evening and night hours after the nuisances of the day (e.g., pesky managers) have gone home.

Even within the high industry standards, Google has taken coffee several notches higher by fostering an avant-garde coffee culture. High-end espresso machines were introduced before the company celebrated its first birthday, hardly the norm for startups at the turn of the 21st century. Today, coffee is available 24/7 in multiple forms throughout the sprawling campus, from drip coffee freshly brewed by highly coveted Clover machines to espresso drinks produced from a variety of semi to fully automatic machines. We Googlers need wander no more than a few yards from our monitors to recharge on caffeine.

Googlers take coffee preparation as seriously as the software we produce. Before you mess around with one of the espresso machines, you are highly encouraged to watch one of the online espresso-preparing tutorials, or attend one of the classes offered by in-house experts. There are no shortage of unspoken rules surrounding coffee preparation. For example, extracting a shot of espresso should take as close to 25 seconds as possible. Going significantly above or below that mark will result in some raised eyebrows from your peers. Thankfully, getting constructive feedback and even compliments about the quality of the crema or foamed milk is also par for the course. Regardless of any Googler's level of mastery, the grinders are off-limits, as only authorized personnel are in charge of setting the grind.

Given these high expectations and exacting standards, it should come as no surprise that selecting coffee beans is not a trivial matter. Recently it has become increasingly clear that the number of quality coffee roasters in the San Francisco Bay Area, home to Google Headquarters, has grown so much that no single person can select the beans for the entire company anymore. In response, Google invited ten roasters of high quality coffee from around the area to show off their beans, serve drinks, and dole out dainty bags of sample beans at an in-house tasting event. Following the event, all of the tasters were asked to complete an online survey. Divergent opinions resulted in the final selection of several roasters to satisfy Googlers' discriminating tastes. For the convenience and benefit of all caffeine-dependent Googlers, an internal web page details the bean supplier at each coffee station around campus.

Of all the espresso machines, one is particularly known for its storied past and ongoing traditions associated with the company's most dedicated group of coffee buffs. It happens to be the machine closest to the office of Google's co-founders, Sergey Brin and Larry Page. Every morning around 9am,

this group of senior Google engineers assembles for a clique cappuccino-making ritual. These are the folks responsible for the fact that millions of queries to Google return answers instantly. They do this by building systems that efficiently access thousands of machines all working in concert. According to the engineers, they have already prepared 16,000 cappuccinos together over the past 15 years (some of them go back even longer to the period they worked together at Digital Equipment Corporation in Palo Alto).

The cappuccino production line is analogous to the processing of the computer programs these engineers develop. They create a pipeline where each takes a specific role in the cappuccino assembly line. One guy packs the ground beans in the portafilter and puts it in the espresso machine. Another takes the brewed espresso to the drink preparation table. Yet another makes sure the perfectly frothed milk arrives just in time to create the cappuccinos. All the while a key person socializes with any other Googlers approaching the machine, thereby providing air cover for his team while they execute. True to their penchant for technical precision as computer scientists, they try to ensure that they not waste any milk or coffee in preparing their drinks.

If you hang around these guys long enough, sooner or later the machine's story will come up. A few years ago, this team realized that a bigger espresso machine with two group heads would greatly enhance the efficiency of their daily cappuccino-making ritual, thereby leaving more time for cutting edge technical discussions. Unfortunately, this argument was not as immediately clear to management as it was to the team. As luck would have it, one day as they were discussing the issue among themselves, a senior executive of the company happened to hover around the coffee area and decided to make it happen. Within just a couple of days, a new and very fancy espresso machine had arrived. However, there were two problems. First, the electrical circuitry could not support the power that this spiffy machine required. In fact, the engineers like to reminisce that the new machine had a higher power rating than the average Google rack of servers at the time. The second problem was that the counter on which the machine was to be placed was too narrow. As yet another testament to the autonomy and efficiency that Googlers enjoy on many fronts, the electrical circuitry was upgraded, a special extension was built for the counter, and coffee preparation resumed within just a few hours.

Brewing technology, paraphernalia, and related skills aside, the espresso machine counters at Google offer an important venue for social interaction. Google is known for growing ideas in bottom-up fashion. Ideas for new services, products or improvements to search come from the engineers and bubble up to management, rather than the other way around. The coffee areas provide a terrific platform for testing new ideas. When you describe an idea, you will almost instantaneously receive some important feedback. Perhaps there is a similar idea brewing somewhere else, or the idea had been tried a while back and failed for reasons that had not yet occurred to you. Or as happens often, your espresso-drinking colleagues will send you away with strong encouragement to build a demo and take the idea to the next step. That's the Google way.

The scene around *the* famed espresso machine at Google at 9am.

Googling Coffee

Millions of people turn to Google several times a day to query for their every need, pro-

1. Denmark

2. Singapore

3. United States

4. Australia

5. New Zealand

6. Netherlands

7. Austria

8. Vietnam

9. Germany

10. Nicaragua

Search volume index

0   100

The chart above shows the top countries querying for "cafés". The chart below shows the top countries querying for "coffee". The darker the country, the more frequent the queries.

1. Papua New Guinea

2. United States

3. Australia

4. Singapore

5. Ethiopia

6. New Zealand

7. Canada

8. Phillipines

9. South Africa

10. Rwanda

Search volume index

0   100

viding Google with an extraordinary resource: a list of all queries submitted to the Google search engine. This query log is the sum of the desires, interests and quests of people from around the world. One can spend a lifetime analyzing the query log, looking for interesting patterns, and trying to understand human behavior. What about coffee? Are people googling coffee? Where? When?

According to Google Insights for Search, a tool that Google offers to answer such questions about its query stream, the most common queries about coffee are for coffee makers and espresso machines, coffee shops and cups, café bars and Internet cafés. The query stream also highlights some cultural differences. For example, in the U.S. and the UK, people seem very interested in coffee tables, while in Sweden and Denmark, Irish coffee is a very common query. In Ethiopia and other coffee-growing countries, queries focus more on coffee production, markets and prices. The fair number of queries about the connection between coffee and health is predominantly expressed with a positive attitude: there are many more queries for health benefits of coffee than risks.

In what countries are people most frequently Googling for coffee? Some of the answers are revealed in the two charts on the previous page displaying the frequency of queries in the query stream. The top chart shows that queries for 'café' are most frequent in Denmark, the United States and the Netherlands. That is, if you took a sample of 1,000 queries coming to Google from Denmark, the word 'café' would occur more frequently than in 1,000 queries coming from any other country. On the other hand, the bottom chart shows that queries for 'coffee' are more frequent in coffee-growing countries like Papua New Guinea and Ethiopia than in other countries. A very clear pattern emerges when inspecting queries for 'espresso.' Apparently, the Greeks search for espresso four times more frequently than the Italians and ten times more frequently than users from any other country. If milk is added back in to the query, the Greeks are less interested. The most frequent queries for "cappuccino" come from Italy and Germany. In the United States, queries about espresso are twice more frequent from Seattle; for cappuccino and coffee in general, Minnesota and the Dakotas have the most interested users.

While all this information may seem to be purely for amusement, valuable insights may be extracted from the data. For example, queries about coffee have very clear seasonal variations and correlations. There is typically a surge in coffee related queries in December and January. For example, in the winter, the frequency of queries about coffee can be up to 30-50% higher than in the summer. This is the kind of golden information that retailers yearn for to justify the extra advertising dollars they spend during that period.

Finally, the analysis also revealed a suspicious statistic: a huge peak in coffee-related queries in June and July of 2005. Was there a crisis in the coffee industry? A new kind of bean that was about to take over the world? Starbucks featured nude baristas? None of the above. A closer investigation corroborates what Web experts would have predicted easily–the surge was somehow linked to sex. In the summer of 2005 people discovered "hot coffee mod" in a hugely popular video game called Grand Auto Theft: San Andreas. Apparently, a special extension for the game can unlock the hot coffee mod. In that mode, the game's character (who was otherwise busy driving around town making a mess) can embark on new kinds of tasks, such as starting to date girlfriends. If he did 'well' on dates, the character would be invited for "coffee" at their place. At that point, other hidden capabilities of the character would come to life. When gamers around the world discovered the extension, they started searching for information about it and most prominently, how to download it. 🍵

Googlers waiting in line for coffee made by baristas from Four Barrel Coffee after a guest lecture on coffee processing. On the right, a frozen yogurt machine and an assortment of in-season Passover food.

THE ORIGINS OF COFFEE

We begin our worldwide search for coffee stories by exploring the historical origins of coffee where facts and legends are inextricably intertwined. The origins of coffee are shrouded in mystery and brim with unanswered questions. The biologists are ahead of the historians in this quest. We know that the Arabica coffee tree originated from Southwestern Ethiopia where it still grows wild today, while its lesser, rougher but sturdier cousin the Robusta comes from Western Africa. Legends suggest that coffee was consumed by the Oromos and other contemporaneous tribes in ancient Ethiopia about 1,500-3,000 years ago, but mostly as a snack, not a drink. The historians are clueless as to why the coffee plant remained unknown to anyone but the ancient Ethiopians until Arabs from Yemen ventured into Ethiopia in the early 15th century in search of ... tea. With such a grim state of knowledge, it comes as no surprise that the legend of Kaldi discovering coffee by watching his prancing goats grew into prominence.

As soon as the Ottoman Empire came into possession of coffee, the precious bean became its symbol. The Turks guarded the waterways from Yemen to ensure control over coffee and brought it to Europe as a weapon of charm. Despite their vigilance, some beans managed to abscond. Brother Baba Budan smuggled seven seeds to India, launching one of the biggest growing regions of the world. The Dutch, who were the maritime superpower in the 17th century, managed to ship the beans to the Island of Reunion (just east of Madagascar) and to the East Indies where they were cultivated further. In a rather circuitous way, the Dutch were also responsible for the arrival of coffee in Central and South America. A coffee plant that they took to the botanical gardens in Amsterdam was gifted to Louis XIV a century later. From there, army captain Gabriel de Clieu who crossed the Atlantic Ocean with a watchful eye on his plant, is said to have heroically brought coffee to the Caribbean and from there to South and Central America, where most of the coffee in the world is grown today. Curiously, as the Ottoman Empire lost its power, the Turks reverted to drinking mostly tea.

Fortunately, a trip to Ethiopia is still a unique experience that offers the opportunity to witness a rich culture that fuses coffee cultivation with consumption, and to inhale a lively sense of pride in the plant that the country has bestowed upon the world. Even though great coffee is also grown in other countries in Eastern Africa, coffee has never earned the same place in peoples' hearts because it was imported by foreign settlers. This section also examines some of the social changes and debates that arose as coffee spread its allure around the globe. The Ottoman Empire was not only a key player in popularizing coffee, but was also the first to face the social challenges that coffee presented.

Coffee ceremony
in Aleta Wondo, Ethiopia–
the pouring of the coffee

ETHIOPIA: The Birthplace of Coffee

ETHIOPIANS WILL TELL YOU THAT STARTING A DAY WITHOUT FOOD is acceptable and sometimes a sad reality, but starting without a cup of coffee (*buna* as they call it) is unfathomable. Coffee is an integral part of Ethiopian daily life, more so than in any other coffee-producing country. While the Ethiopian coffee ceremony may conjure up a very formal event, it actually takes place quite casually several times a day, practically every time coffee is consumed. Unlike most coffee consumers who purchase roasted or even ground beans from their markets, Ethiopian markets sell only green beans. Coffee preparation involves roasting the beans on the spot, grinding with a pestle, boiling in water, and then consuming the brew at a leisurely pace. The unique part of the ceremony is when the roaster brings the smoking hot roasted beans up to each guests' face, whereupon coffee clouds waft into the guests' nostrils and impart the spiritual blessing of coffee. Coffee gatherings form the backbone of Ethiopian society, whether in or outside the home, and especially at rituals of birth, marriage and death.

Coffee culture is deeply ingrained in Ethiopia. The country is dependent on its coffee industry, which comprises 60% of all exports and accounts for a large source of its foreign currency reserve. Ethiopians consume half of the coffee they produce. This is a country that has not only a special government ministry for coffee and tea, but also a premier soccer club named *Ethiopia Coffee*. The club is funded directly by a special tax levied from coffee growers, millers and exporters. In no other country in the world do the cultures of impassioned coffee production and consumption weave together so poignantly.

A mural of Kaldi and his goats in a coffee academy in Seoul, South Korea

Roasting coffee for a traditional coffee ceremony in Sidama, Ethiopia

Although no one disputes Ethiopia as the birthplace of coffee, how coffee was discovered continues to be unraveled by modern research. As with many details in the history of coffee, the boundaries among legends and facts are blurred at best.

Classical legend centers on Kaldi, a goat herdsman and a poet at heart. As Kaldi was urging his goats home one day, he noticed that his herd was possessed by a mysterious new wave of energy that propelled them to prance around giddily. Upon closer investigation, he saw that they were chewing on a type of red cherry he had never seen before. He tried some of that cherry, and was soon dancing with his goats. More conservative versions of the legend have Kaldi waiting a day to verify that none of his goats had died from the cherries before tasting the cherries himself.

The second part of the legend involves a preacher who happened by while Kaldi was bouncing with his goats. The lively scene inspired him to partake in the cherries. He immediately noticed the jolting effect and decided to give some to his congregants who were having difficulties staying awake during his sermons. That worked so well that he soon became known as an electrifying speaker who could keep his congregants up all night.

There is also a more culinary version of the legend. Kaldi brought some cherries to a holy man in a nearby monastery. At first, the holy man disapproved of the cherries and threw them into the fire. But when their irresistible aroma wafted through the air, he rushed to rake them from the embers, ground them up, and put them into a glass of hot water—thus producing the first coffee drink.

More careful historical analysis and research give the somewhat indirect credit for discovering coffee to the most inconceivable of all, the tea-loving Chinese! Between 1405 and 1433, Emperor Yongle of the Ming Dynasty dispatched seven treasure fleets from China into the Indian Ocean. Comprising of hundreds of vessels, the treasure fleets were spectacularly impressive. They carried from China goods

An Ethiopian husk shower. The husks are separated from the coffee beans, collected into bags, and later used as wood chips for heating.

such as silks, porcelain and of course, tea. They brought back to China exquisite plants and animals from the voyage, including a giraffe for the Emperor to marvel at.

Some of these vessels ended up in the Port of Aden in Yemen and helped expose the locals to brewing tea leaves in boiling water. The Yemenites liked the effect tea had on them. When the last of the missions returned to China, the Yemenites (in particular the Sufis who had been exposed to tea during their own visits to China) started looking for a local plant that would produce similar effects, but to no avail. They broadened their search by hopping over the narrow passage on the Red Sea into Abyssinia (as Ethiopia was known at the time), where they found the leaf of the coffee plant as a tea substitute. Soon after, they discovered that they could make an even better drink from the pulp of the coffee cherry known as *qisher*, a drink that is still consumed today among Yemenites. Finally, they discovered the powers of the coffee bean itself, whose appeal became apparent only after roasting. Because the identity of the first explorer who journeyed into Abyssinia and discovered the coffee plant remains a mystery, the frolicsome and upbeat Kaldi legends have taken root and spread far and wide.

From a botanical perspective, we are on more solid ground. Coffee first grew (and still grows) wild in the fertile highlands of Kaffa, in Southwestern Ethiopia. Scanty evidence seems to identify the first true coffee lovers as the nomadic Galla and Oromo tribes who lived in Abyssinia about 1,500 to 3,000 years ago. The Oromos actually used the beans as snacks. They crushed the beans and combined them with animal fat to create snacks the size of golf balls. The Oromos were particularly fond of eating these snacks just before battle. Unfortunately, their caffeinated weapon proved more unique than effective because the Oromos were often defeated by the Bongas, who were expert slave traders. The Bongas' victories led the Oromos to suffer the fate of slaves. As they were transported to other parts of Ethiopia, the Oromos brought their coffees with them.

One of the new destinations was the city of Harar in the eastern part of Ethiopia, on the main trade route to Yemen. Coffee was first cultivated in Harar sometime during the 1500-year window. The coffee bean was revered in Harar and the city was named after the caste of coffee growers, the Harash. In an early nod to intellectual property protection, city officials had prohibited the Harash from leaving Harar for fear that the secret of their precious art of coffee cultivation would leak to the outside world.

The role of coffee in Abyssnia is as rich as the tapestry of tribes making up the country's population. Coffee was a common subject of the Oromo prayers:

coffeepot give us peace
coffeepot let children grow
let our wealth swell
please protect us from evil
give us rain and grass

Grinding the beans with a pestle

The Oromos and their neighboring Gallas created elaborate ceremonies around coffee called *bun-qualle*, to celebrate sex and death. In these ceremonies, coffee beans replaced fatted oxen as sacrifices to the gods. The obvious resemblance of the coffee bean to the female sex organ inspired one of these ceremonies. This particular ceremony was always held after a night of abstinence. After the beans were husked, they were stirred in butter with a stick called *dannaba*, the Oromo word for penis. Since some people could not imagine that a dead piece of wood can impart life, they replaced the *dannaba* with bundles of living grass. As the coffee beans were stirred to the sound of another prayer, coffee fruits burst open from the heat. This bursting (better known in modern coffee nomenclature as the first or second crack) was a symbol of both childbirth and of the last cry of a dying man. At this point, the following prayer was recited:

Ashama, my coffee, burst open to bring peace
there you opened your mouth
please wish me peace
keep far from me all evil tongues

In being eaten, the coffee beans died, blessing new thought and life. The main event, which could be a wedding, circumcision, or another similarly adventurous activity, then took place.

Fast forward to present day Ethiopia. Unlike others in Africa, this is a country that has remained independent of foreign colonizers. Much of the ancient and indigenous cultures remain intact today: The Oromos and the Bongas still clash from time to time, mostly over water sources for their cattle; cattle herders in Southern Ethiopia still leave for long journeys equipped with snacks made of coffee cherries roasted in butter.

To gain an up close and personal glimpse of today's Ethiopian coffee culture, I visited the Sidama Region in Southern Ethiopia. After spending years seeking out and enjoying the much-coveted Sidama and neighboring Yirga Cheffe coffees in cafés around the world, the trip to this region felt like an overdue pilgrimage. The Common River program in the town of Aleta Wondo, a community development program run by a U.S.-based nonprofit organization, offered a candid view of the lives of Ethiopian farmers today.

I reached Aleta Wondo with the kind help of Fisseha Cherenet, a coffee expert who has built many of the coffee mills in the Sidama region and owns two mills of his own. The seven-hour drive south from Addis Ababa began with crossing the arid Great Rift Valley and then reaching the relatively modern city of Awassa, gateway to Sidama. Continuing south from Awassa on the road to Kenya, the drive was punctuated with frequent crossings of cattle and (non-giddy) goats; numerous and typically inactive makeshift government checkpoints; legions of peddlers offering papaya, mango and bananas; and people strolling down the main road as if it were their own backyard. Coffee fields that were typically shaded by banana trees lined both sides of the road.

An hour south of Awassa, a dirt road forked to the left of the main road, leading ultimately to Somalia. A bumpy 17 kilometer drive on that road brought us to Aleta Wondo, a village of about 14,000 people that is completely dedicated to coffee farming and processing. The highly acclaimed coffees of Aleta Wondo, many of which are grown at altitudes of more than 2000 meters, are known for their refreshing acidity, floral notes, lingering sweetness, as well as exotic fruit tones (such as jasmine and bergamot orange) in the aftertaste.

The Common River Project was co-founded in 2007 by Fisseha's cousin Tsegaye Bekele, a native of Aleta Wondo, and Donna Sillan, an international public health consultant who had trained communities in over 35 countries in preventative healthcare for over three

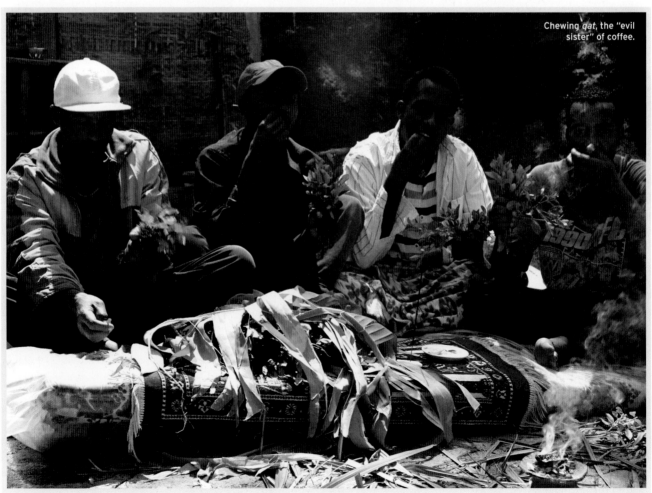

Chewing *qat*, the "evil sister" of coffee.

A classroom in Common River, Aleta Wondo.

decades. Tsegaye and Donna are both longtime residents of Mill Valley, a town in Northern California of about the same size and with similar topography and weather as Aleta Wondo. The two met in 2006 at the local Peet's Coffee shop and much to their surprise, discovered that Donna's two godchildren had just been adopted from Tsegaye's hometown!

A few years earlier, Tsegaye had visited Aleta Wondo for the first time in forty years and was struck by the changes that had taken place during that period. The country's population had exploded from 20 million to over 80 million. Conditions in his hometown were horrendous. Classrooms in the local schools overflowed with children, often with more than 100 per class. Due to malaria, TB and AIDS, there was an alarming number of orphaned children. Since Donna had decided to focus her efforts and provide continuity and increased impact on a single community, it was natural for her to join forces with Tsegaye and try to help the community for which they shared a common passion.

Tsegaye's family, who were among the founders of Aleta Wondo, had owned a sizable plot of land in town. Like many other properties, that land was confiscated during the Derg Regime following the ouster of the long time emperor Haile Selassie who reigned from 1974 to 1991. Tsegaye succeeded in persuading the officials of Aleta Wondo to return his land by promising to use it for the benefit of the community.

Under their leadership, the Project has funded the construction of four classrooms in a compound on the outskirts of Aleta Wondo and set up an educational program. Admission to the school now numbers 130 children and is decided by a committee, with preference given to orphans or vulnerable children of local coffee farmers. They plan to grow the school by building one more classroom every year. The entire operation is funded by proceeds of coffee sales and charitable donations. Common River also includes a school lunch program that often provides the children their only nutritious meal of the day. Most of the food comes from a traditional demonstration garden and a small herd of cows on the premises. On weekend afternoons, the classrooms are filled with illiterate women learning to read and write for the first time.

Until two years ago, Donna and Tsegaye were able to export Aleta Wondo coffee directly from Ethiopia and obtain prices commensurate with its award-winning quality. However, in 2009 the Ethiopian government created the Ethiopian Commodities Exchange (ECX), a clearing house for all export coffees. Without a special export permit, farmers are now required to export their coffee through the ECX where all coffees are dumped into one of nine quality grades. This makes it extremely difficult to distinguish among the rich variety of Ethiopian coffees. To obtain an export license, an individual farmer must have at least thirty contiguous hectares on one farm, a virtually impossible bar to meet in the regions of Sidama and Yirga Cheffe. These restrictions have become great barriers for

Greeters at the entrance to Yirga Cheffe, a legendary coffee region in southern Ethiopia

specialty roasters to develop direct trade relationships with specific farmers who provide the highest quality beans and for consumers to trace the origins of their coffee.

In a country where most people survive on barely one dollar a day, the main challenge facing Ethiopian coffee farmers today is the vicious cycle of poverty. Because an average farmer in Ethiopia may earn less than $400 per year, farmers lack the resources to invest in their farms. This in turn results in yields that are extremely low compared to their peers' in other coffee-producing countries. For example, a typical farm in Ethiopia produces 2-5 quintals (boxes of 100kg) per hectare, whereas farmers in Costa Rica may produce up to 35 quintals from the same land.

To make matters worse, coffee is also facing some stiff competition from *qat*, known as the "evil sister" of coffee. Qat (pronounced "chat" in Ethiopia) is an amphetamine-like stimulant that causes euphoria when chewed. Qat also suppresses the chewer's hunger, which is another reason for its addictive powers in this impoverished region of the world. Unfortunately, chewing qat leaves one with little desire to do anything else, such as work. Consequently, a large portion of the younger population is becoming addicts who are unproductive members of society. Qat is illegal in many parts of the world, but not in East Africa.

Qat has given coffee its run for the money. The streets of Sidama and the Yirga Cheffe regions are lined with peddlers offering bundles of qat to every passing car. The export of qat to neighboring Somalia and Djibouti has become big business. In the earlier days, qat had lost out to coffee because its leaves did not produce as appealing a drink as that of the coffee bush and its quality deteriorated more quickly after being picked. Now that qat can be transported by air to its eager consumers around East Africa, it has become a much more attractive option for farmers. From the farmers' perspective, qat is easier to grow (assuming water is plentiful), less complicated to process, and may be harvested four times a year and sold without the hassles of the ECX.

Despite the myriad socioeconomic problems plaguing the country, Ethiopian coffees remain prized on the world market and the related culture unparalleled in its uniqueness. The coffee ceremonies I sat through left me with this lasting impression: even though the roasting and grinding methods used were the simplest imaginable, the resulting cup was always amazingly bright, bold, and flavorful. ☙

THE OTTOMAN EMPIRE: Passing the Coffee Baton to Europe

ACCORDING TO LEGEND, THE PROPHET MOHAMMED SAID that the influence of coffee could propel him to *"unhorse forty men and possess forty women."* With such gallant endorsement, it comes as no surprise that coffee played a very significant role in the Ottoman Empire. However, it was not always a smooth sailing love fest. At certain times, those caught drinking coffee in Constantinople might have been beaten to death or thrown into the Bosphorus River. In Cairo, on the other hand, a husband's failure to provide enough coffee for his wife could have been grounds for divorce.

One of the biggest mysteries of coffee history is why it took so long for the bean to come out of Ethiopia, especially given that Ethiopia was well-known to foreign traders. As we described in the previous chapter, the big break came in the early 15th century when Arabs crossed the narrow passage over the Red Sea in their search for a leaf that could replace the tea to which they had grown accustomed, courtesy of the Chinese treasure fleets that visited Yemen.

Who exactly found coffee in the 15th century is another mystery. Legend tells of the Sufi al-Shadhili of Mocha, master of the Shadhilya order, who first noticed the power of coffee and used it to keep his dervishes alert. There are many stories about how al-Shadhili stumbled upon coffee, some even placing him at the scene of another legend with Kaldi and his goats. Because the Sufis had been exposed to tea during their visits to China, it is likely that when the Chinese fleets stopped coming to Yemen, they sought a replacement with more alacrity than their fellow countrymen. The Sufis, described as both the *"inner mystical dimension of Islam"* and the *"hippies of Islam,"* were also the first to start using coffee in their ceremonies. They would begin their long nights of prayer by passing coffee held in a red vessel from hand to hand and sipping from it. This ceremony not only raised eyebrows but landed them in trouble later when the legality of coffee came to be challenged.

The appearance of coffee in Yemen was marked by two other important developments in the annals of coffee. First, the Arabic word for wine, *qahwa*, was initially used for coffee. Since Islam forbids alcohol, the word was put to a different use. Second, al-Shadhilli is said to have been the first to make a coffee drink from the beans. Up until then, the Ethiopians had either chewed the bean or made a drink from the leaves of the coffee plant or the pulp surrounding the bean. Sufi al-Shadhilli actually boiled the bean. It was probably not as tasty as you might imagine, because this far predated the practice of roasting coffee beans. In keeping with Yemenite tradition, an assortment of spices was added to the drink to spruce up its taste.

The empire played a pivotal role in spreading coffee across the world. The Ottomans occupied Yemen as early as about 1400. During its heyday they controlled the Port of Mocha from which coffee was shipped to other parts of the empire. As we recount in subsequent chapters, they introduced

Turgay Yildizli, the Turkish competitor at the 2011 Cezve/Ibrik World Championship

coffee to France in style via a Turkish ambassador, unintentionally left bags of beans behind in Vienna as they fled from their failed siege on the city, and in due time, addicted the entire Adriatic Coast to the bean.

As "early adopters" of coffee, the Ottomans were the first to confront social upheaval in the communities that were becoming dependent on the stimulant. Because coffee was a social lubricant, some rulers felt threatened by the culture emerging around coffee and the related opportunities it offered their subjects. These rulers tried to ban coffee and coffeehouses by invoking Islamic principles. The first of these rulers was Kha'ir Beg, head of the Mecca police. In 1511, he realized that the source of certain satirical verses about him was folks getting together to drink coffee. He immediately called a "hearing" on the legality of coffee that included experts on the topic. Proponents of the ban argued that because coffee is intoxicating, it is therefore against the principles of Islam. They pointed to the Sufi's practice of passing the coffee vessel from hand to hand and the red color of the vessel as symbols of such impropriety. Coffee fans countered that whatever is not explicitly outlawed by Islam is fair play. Furthermore, they argued that according to the laws of Islam, intoxication is defined to cause inability to *distinguish between a man and a woman,"* which was not yet within the purview of coffee drinks. Kha'ir Beg did not take a chance on the outcome of this debate. He arranged two doctors as his main witnesses who ensured a hearing outcome in his favor. Coffee was then banned in Mecca, and anyone caught drinking coffee whipped on the spot.

This was just the beginning of the story. Kha'ir Beg was unaware that Kansuh al-Ghawri, his royal superior and the Sultan of Cairo, had

A café in the old city of Jerusalem

already become hooked on coffee. When al-Ghawri received the report on the ban, he quickly dismissed it. Although Kha'ir Beg applied the ban, the tacit support from Cairo inspired coffee lovers in Mecca to continue drinking in private. Kha'ir Beg was removed from his position the following year. Interestingly, even when coffeehouses were being banned, home consumption was being encouraged. In 1523, a covenant was introduced to the marriage contract in Cairo stipulating that a husband must provide his wife with an adequate supply of coffee. Failure to do so could constitute grounds for divorce.

Over time, the quandaries of coffee, inebriation and prayer came to be resolved by changing the morning routine. Muslims started drinking coffee after the morning prayer rather than before. That way, it could not be argued that the religious activity was in any way affected by the intoxicating effects of coffee. In fact, the Turkish word for breakfast is *kahvalti*, which literally means "before coffee," reinforcing the morning order.

By the middle of the 16th century, coffeehouses had populated every major city in the Ottoman Empire. Two Syrian businessmen, Hakam and Shams, introduced coffeehouses to Istanbul in 1555. Known at the time as Constantinople, Istanbul was the center of political, business and intellectual activity of the Ottoman Empire. With the juxtaposition of the splendors of the Empire and extreme poverty, it was a city of extremes. Unlike previous coffeehouses that were associated with Sufi gatherings, the coffeehouses in Istanbul were purely secular social venues. People gathered to discuss the politics of the day, enjoy literature and poetry, conduct business dealings, and exchange gossip. Men came to drink and smoke. After a while, coffeehouses started to offer other pleasures including coffees infused with interesting combinations of drugs (opium and saffron), hash mixed with tobacco and *"beautiful boyes who serves as stales [prostitutes]."* In short, these houses of pleasure were not exactly the vision that Kha'ir Beg had in mind.

The happening place that was Istanbul attracted many foreign visitors. This led to the first Western accounts of coffee culture. The best known is from George Sandys who visited the English ambassador for a few months in 1610. Sandys was a regular at high powered social gatherings in London and as such a frequent visitor to taverns. Sandys started looking for the same in Istanbul, and noted:

> *"Although they are destitute of Taverns, yet have they Coffa-houses, which something resemble them. There sit they chatting most of the day; and sippe of a drinke called Coffa (of the berry that is made of) in little China dishes, as hot as they can suffer it: black as soote and tasting not much unlike it."*

The secularization of coffee did not signal an end to its troubles. Murad IV, who ruled from 1623 to 1640, became the most violent opponent of coffee. He banned coffee around 1633. Anyone caught having coffee endured beatings. Anyone caught a second time was sewn into a leather bag and thrown into the Bosphorus River to drown. In fact, according to foreign eyewitness accounts, Murad even wandered the streets with his executioner and killed anyone he caught drinking coffee or smoking. As a result of his ban and the harsh punishments, many coffee merchants fanned out to France, Italy and Austria. The ban was lifted after Murad IV died, but lasting damage to the coffee scene in Istanbul had already been done. Despite the persecutions, coffee survived in Arab societies as it provided a social stimulant like no other. However, coffee culture never regained its mid-16th century glory. After the Ottoman Empire lost its power, much of the Arab world shifted back to tea leaves whose search had led to the discovery of coffee in the 15th century. ✎

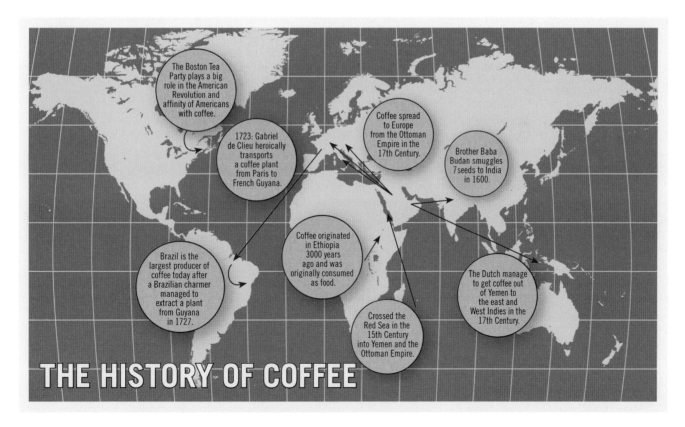

EUROPE

For a coffee culturalist, Europe is paradise. From its venerable history, prismatic local cultures, grand cafés that stand side by side with infinitely charming ones, to the coterie of young coffee enthusiasts who are pushing coffee culture to new heights, no other continent offers a fuller smorgasbord of coffee experiences.

In early 17th century Europe, coffee was a mere curiosity and used mostly by the upper class as a pharmaceutical. By the middle of that century, the Turks had quickly spread coffee throughout the continent. They unintentionally left coffee beans behind as they fled from their failed siege of Vienna, seduced the Parisians with elaborate parties, sold coffee on the streets of Venice, and opened cafés in London .

Europe swiftly developed a spirited café culture where the political controversies of the day were debated, financial transactions were conducted, art and literature were created, and endless opportunities for impassioned rendezvous were fervently pursued and meticulously documented. It is hardly astonishing that coffee became a harbinger of broadscale social sea change on a continent where water was so polluted that the average person (and child) had little choice but to drink beer for breakfast, lunch and dinner. Coffeehouses provided a novel environment to socialize where, in addition to maintaining sobriety, mental alacrity was enhanced by coffee. Conversations started flowing and made more sense, logic rose to the forefront, ideas flourished, and even revolutions were schemed.

Today you can still experience some of the tradition-bound and lore-filled grand cafés in major European cities including Vienna, Paris, Barcelona, Prague, Venice, and Zurich. You can step farther back in time by lingering in the cafés of Sarajevo, Bosnia where you might delight in being transported into a Turkish café in Istanbul circa 1550. To witness the latest and greatest in the coffee world, visit London, Oslo, Stockholm, Copenhagen, and even Reykjavík where recent World Barista Champions and their cohorts are shaping the specialty coffee scene.

Only a short flight from Europe, Israel offers unrivaled insight into the harmonious juxtaposition of ancient and modern coffee cultures.

EUROPA
1989

Copenhagen, Denmark

VIENNA: Decadent Party at the End of the Century

LEOPOLD HAWELKA, WHO CELEBRATED HIS 100TH BIRTHDAY ON APRIL 11, 2011, dresses up in a suit and bow tie every morning and walks the few blocks between his home and the café bearing his name. He takes his honorary seat next to the bar, greets the customers, and banters with and complains to the staff for a few hours. Leopold does not work at the café anymore. His son Gunter, a more recent pensioner of 70 years young, and his grandchildren Amir and Michael have taken over. The Hawelkas are assisted by a very dedicated staff that, like many café staff in Vienna, considers their jobs as lifetime employment. A tuxedoed server at Café Hawelka proudly revealed that he had waited three years until his predecessor retired before landing his job. Café Hawelka is one of the most well known Viennese coffeehouses that had reigned supreme as a literary and artistic café during much of the last century. Along with the grand Viennese cafés that flourished during the *"fin de sciecle,"* it epitomizes not only one of the great European coffeehouse traditions but also nostalgic reminiscences of Vienna's historically significant role in shaping the coffee culture of Europe.

Coffee did not arrive in Vienna as the result of a friendly prearranged business transaction. Ask any student in Austria how coffee arrived here, and they will tell the story of the Siege of Vienna. In the summer of 1683, the Turkish Ottoman forces besieged Vienna in their attempt to extend their reach in Europe. On September 12, the Battle of Vienna erupted as the Ottomans closed in on the city. Fortunately for the Austrians, they managed to turn the tide in their favor with last minute help from forces led by King John Sobieski of Poland, among others. As the Turks fled hastily in retreat, they left behind treasures that included camels, sheep, tents, and most signif-

Café Sperl

icantly, bags of beans. In their euphoria, the Austrians thought the bags of green beans were camel food.

Fortunately, a Pole named Franz Kolschitsky who had spied behind the Ottoman lines during the siege knew better. Otherwise, I would probably be starting to recite the legend of Reinhard and his prancing camels. Kolschitsky asked to keep the sacks of coffee as a token of appreciation for his work during the Siege. A couple of years later he opened the first coffeehouse in Vienna, called the Blue Bottle (now the name of a trendy café in San Francisco). Upon discovering the Austrians' distaste for particles in their drinks, he began the practice of filtering coffee. As with any detail concerning coffee history, there are disagreements about Kolschitsky's exact role in the war and the degree of his chutzpah when he requested the bags of beans.

The siege on Vienna birthed another major contribution to the culinary world. A Viennese baker named Peter Wender discovered one day when he was working in the basement of a bakery, that the Turks were digging tunnels under the city. After notifying the city officials, he

Leopold Hawelka

felt he should take credit for the tip by baking and selling breads in the shape of the crescent, the Ottmon symbol. The breads, called *pfizers*, became popular following the defeat of the Ottomans. A century later, the Viennese princess Marie Antoinette asked her servants to bake pfizers after she moved to Paris to become queen. The French added a generous amount of butter and some yeast, and the croissant was born. Hence, when millions of Europeans breakfast on a coffee and croissant every morning, they are experiencing a most politically loaded meal: the coffee celebrating the Turkish contribution to Europe and the croissant that was created to celebrate their defeat.

The Viennese like to claim that they shaped the coffee culture of Europe. To some extent, they are right. If not for the Viennese influence, Europe may still be drinking Turkish coffee, or some horrible substitute. Whether the tradition of sweetening coffee with milk and cream began in Vienna or Venice is subject to debate. It is likely that both places began this practice simultaneously. It was definitely not a Turkish idea, as the Turks were somewhat lactose intolerant and believed that combining coffee and milk could cause leprosy.

The classical Viennese coffeehouse is a place to meet friends, read the newspaper, discuss business, enjoy a game of pool, chess, or poker, and of course, indulge in a variety of tempting strudels and specialty house cakes. Coffeehouses had long ago become incredibly fascinating and attractive places for the intellectual, artistic, scientific, economic and political elite to see and be seen. It is a small wonder that the Viennese coffeehouse tradition has been imitated in many other countries.

The signature drink of Vienna is the *mélange*, which is basically a combination of coffee (possibly espresso) and foam or milk. The

Maria Theresia is a signature Viennese lady's coffee drink that is prepared with cointreau or grand marnier.

The highlight of my Vienna coffee search was interviewing the Hawelkas over two of their specialty drinks, the Hawelka mélange and a Maria Theresia with grand marnier, at the cozy and fabled Café Hawelka. While the golden years of the café may have passed, it is the outside world that has succumbed to changes brought on by modernity, not the café that has survived as a timeless haven through the loyalty of its regulars and the curiosity of tourists. One wall is covered with old posters advertising exhibitions, concerts and lectures. The other walls showcase a collection of artwork by the café's more talented customers of yesteryear.

Leopold was short on the specifics of history, but ebullient with humor. When asked whether he would be willing to entertain a few questions, he responded: "*Sure, but let's go home, it's cheaper there.*" Once my wife and I ordered a few drinks, he became more relaxed and the jokes veered away from concerns over coffeehouse revenues. When I asked for a cappuccino, his son quickly whispered : "*Say mélange, not cappuccino. Same thing but dad doesn't like the Italian names.*" I enjoyed my first mélange made with Ethiopian coffee along with the house apricot cake that was served piping hot from the oven by their Cambodian kitchen helper. When the subject of coffee books came up, the Hawelkas proudly brought out *Hawelka Mélange*, their book about the café, which Leopold deftly "autographed" for us with a coffee cup doodle.

Gunter Hawelka was happy to talk and answer questions, including detailed explanations of Viennese coffee culture vis-à-vis the French and Italian. Café Hawelka opened in 1905 as the first American bar in Vienna, appropriately named *Je T'aime*. After World War I, it was taken over by Ludwig Karl. Shortly after Leopold bought the café in 1939, he was drafted to serve in the Austrian army for a five-year term that took him to Poland, Russia, Hungary, Italy and the battle of La Rochelle in France. His wife Josefine was pregnant with Gunter during the time and had to close the café. Café Hawelka reopened after WWII in 1945. Gunter remembers that when he was very young, his parents used to split the shifts at the café. His mom used to work the night shift and had quick chats with Leopold when he came on duty at 5am.

Coffee and cake at Café Landtmann in Vienna

Gunter was trained as a pastry chef in the rough setting of the Ritz Hotel in Paris, and then spent time in London. He refers to himself as a chronic secondhand smoker, but argues that smoking is an integral part of the café atmosphere. Perhaps the reason he cannot imagine banning smoking in the café is the story told by his mom: When the café reopened after the war, the Hawelkas waited anxiously for their first customers. A man finally came in and asked for coffee, which Josefine was happy to serve. But then he asked whether they also had cigarettes. When the answer was no, he left claiming that he had no choice but to drink his coffee elsewhere.

Because cigarettes were difficult to come by after the war due to strict government regulations, a black market naturally developed around cigarette trading. Realizing how critical it was to have cigarettes on hand at the café, the Hawelkas decided to participate in the thriving trade. When the same customer came back a while later and asked for coffee, Josefine replied: "*Yes. And we have cigarettes too.*"

Josefine, who died in 2005, was a compassionate owner with a keen business sense. She

Café Hawelka

Café Central, Vienna

A politically loaded breakfast: the coffee that the Turks left behind in Vienna and the croissant that was created to mock them.

would often give patrons of the starving artist profile a month of free coffee in exchange for their artwork. The walls of the café became gradually adorned by these creations. Over the years, the café has enjoyed the company of many famous patrons, from Grace Kelly, Henry Miller, Egon Schiele, Richard Burton, Nobel Prize winning author Elias Canetti, to the Austrian do-it-all, Arnold Schwarzenegger.

For more wartime stories, venture slightly out of the center of town to the more extravagant Café Sperl. The spacious chamber on the right has a table with newspapers spread over it for the customers' perusing pleasure. Several billiard tables adorn the back portion of the chamber. A collection of paintings created in the café, now called the Sperl Collection, is housed in a Viennese museum. There is even an old-style phone booth to complete the retro mood. According to the owner's son Rainer Staub, students from the nearby technical university had made the calculations for the Austrian artillery forces in this café. He joked, *"that may well have contributed to the Austrians' defeat."* The expansiveness of the café did not go unnoticed by the Russians occupying Vienna after World War II, when they used the café as a holding place for their horses.

While anecdotes of the 20th century focus mostly on the wars, the Viennese coffee scene at the end of the 19th century was an ecstatic party scene. The *"fin de siecle"* coincided with the peak of the Viennese coffee culture, the period when Sigmund Freud was redefining sexual desire as the primary motivational energy of human life, Gustav Klimt was painting *"The Kiss"* and other works marked by frank eroticism, and the Klimt-mentored young Egon Schiele was gaining notoriety for artwork spotlighting erotic, pornographic and often disturbing subjects.

Café Landtmann, the oldest surviving café in Vienna, dates back to 1873 and is an elegant institution that exemplifies that decadently intense and exhilarating period. Conveniently situated across the street from Vienna University and City Hall, this lavishly decorated grand café is a common gathering place for students and politicians alike. This legendary café has been and continues to be one of the most popular in Vienna. Its list of famous patrons include Sigmund Freud (known to have scheduled patient sessions there), Gustav Mahler, Marlene Dietrich, Burt Lancaster, Hillary Rodham Clinton, and Sir Paul McCartney.

A short walk from the Landtmann, not nearly long enough to burn off the pastry calories just consumed, is Café Central. With its soaring vaulted ceilings, opulent decor, first-rate cakes and strudels, phantoms of former regulars, and piano favorites, Café Central is not only a landmark café but also the embodiment of the formal Viennese coffeehouses. Upon entry, patrons are immediately transported to the end of the 19th century and embraced by its exuberance. Established in 1906, the café is located very close to the Imperial Palace, Stephens Cathedral and the State Opera. It was the focal point of Europe's intellectual elite and a meeting place for revolutionaries until the middle of the 20th century. Sigmund Freud used to come here to play chess, as did Leon Trotsky during one of his exiles from Russia. Though these and others were respected figures, the patron saint of Café Central was Peter Altenberg, an Austrian writer and poet known as a *"bohemian's Bohemian."* Altenberg's life-sized statue sits by the table at the entrance and greets every patron. Altenberg literally called this place home—the café was listed as his address on his calling card. And he needed it. Altenberg was typically short on money and often had to rely on charm to get others to pay for his meals and coffee. 🖎

PARIS: The Caffeinated Revolution

"Artaud, I knew, was a sick, tormented madman, and I was interested in him, but not humanly; and he, being so morbid and so hypersensitive, also wanted the trophy which he knew Allendy, Henry and Eduardo claimed ... Sitting in the Coupole, we kissed and I tried to prove to Artaud that I was sincere, that I was a divided being, that this was not a game, but a tragedy—because I could not love imaginatively and humanly at the same time."

These sensuous words of the French-Cuban erotica author Anaïs Nin are perhaps an extreme illustration of the spirit of the coffee scene in Paris, but they do provide a flavor for the life of the literati who used to grace the cafés of the city. Nin wrote this passage in the early 1930's at Café Le Coupole, one of the landmarks of the Montparnasse neighborhood of Paris where she often sat with her partner Henry James. Montparnasse enjoyed its heyday in the period between the two world wars. Being one of the more affordable neighborhoods of Paris, it was attractive to the likes of Pablo Picasso who left his Montmartre studio to come here, Marc Chagall who came from Russia, Amadeo Modigliani who came from Italy, and Leon Trotsky and Igor Stravinsky who transplanted themselves here from Café Central in Vienna.

Even the Parisians would probably agree that in this highly-charged café culture, the quality of coffee has always been of secondary concern. It would not be fair to fault the French—none of their colonies grew Arabica beans, only Robusta. They simply learned to make up for the deficiency with a refined pastry culture and unrivaled ambiance. Fueled by the extra kick provided by Robusta, Paris illustrates the transformative power of coffee on European culture better than any other city, not to mention the direct path from cafés to a revolution.

The first attempts to introduce coffee to Paris failed for the simple reason that cafés were too ordinary, too down-to-earth. To attract the attention of Parisians, style and allure have always been requisite. Turkish ambassador Soliman Aga succeeded in indulging these debonair sensibilities of the French. During the years leading up to the 1683 Turkish siege on Vienna, the Turks sought to ensure that the French would not interfere with their plans. Soliman Aga began a concerted diplomatic serenade that involved inviting members of the French elite, one by one, for a soirée at his residence. These assemblies began with lavish pampering in grand Turkish style. The guests were washed in rosewater while burning myrrh perfumed their faces. They were then treated to a coffee ceremony that involved the roasting, pounding and brewing of coffee, and enjoying the potion served in fancy demitasse cups. Before long, these exclusive affairs became the most sought after invitations among the French glitterati, culminating in a meeting with King Louis XIV where he signed an anti-aggression treaty. The Turks' defeat in Vienna put a temporary dent in the adoption of coffee in France. That was but a minor detail in the grand scheme of the coffee annals.

The brilliant entrepreneur of the day was a Sicilian named Francesco Procopio dei Coltelli who had taken to heart the earlier failure of the simple cafés and decided to capitalize on the elites' fascination with Aga's extravagant parties. In 1686, Coltelli opened up Le Pro-

The café scene in Montparnasse

cope, whose focus was more on pomp and circumstance, and less on the coffee. Coltelli installed in the café an entire bathhouse with large wall mirrors and marble-topped tables, a style that later pervaded many other cafés in Europe. Fortunately for him, a few years later the Comedie Francaise moved in across the street, thereby expanding its regular clientele to include Molière and Racine. The café's most celebrated patron was Voltaire, the French writer and philosopher who was one of the main forces behind the French Enlightenment (and was known for drinking 50 cups of coffee a day, the equivalent of 12 liters). Voltaire was not alone at Le Procope. Other well-known patrons included Napoleon, Rousseau, and its favorite American, Benjamin Franklin. With these luminaries, Le Procope became the center of intellectual life in Paris in the 18th century. Today, Le Procope is more of a restaurant

for tourists than a café. It has also upgraded its services to include wireless Internet access.

When coffee first arrived on the Parisian scene, some predicted that it would be no more than a fad. Coffee was a subject of some intense medical debate between those who claimed it *"dried up the cerebrospinal fluid and the convolutions ... the upshot being general exhaustion, paralysis and impotence"* instead of those who claimed it *"sweetened"* the lower bowel and was able to *"breaketh wind and openeth any stopping."* This particular fascination with clearing stoppings was one of the few benefits of Robusta, which is higher in caffeine than Arabica and therefore more adept at producing such effects. Like in other European countries, coffee ultimately prevailed even before its medicinal effects were fully fleshed out.

With all due respect to the bowels, coffee provided a much more important intellectual stimulant in Paris. The café was a venue where people of any class could gather and freely discuss the issues of the day, in a much more attractive atmosphere than pubs. As the food writer Margaret Visser wrote: *"Men and women could, without impropriety, consort as they had never done before. They could meet in public places and talk."* Honore de Balzac, one of the best-known French novelists of the 19th century who enjoyed taking his coffee black and strong, captures one of the most vivid accounts of the effects of coffee on the thinkers and writers of the day: *"Everything becomes agitated; ideas are set in motion like army battalions on the battlefields, and then the battle begins. Memories charge forward, banners flying; the light cavalry of comparisons progresses at magnificent gallop; the artillery of logic hastens into the fray with its cannons and cartridges."*

It comes as no surprise then that the French Enlightenment which espoused logic and reason in decision-making and sowed the seeds of the French and American revolutions was rooted in the cafés. On July 12, 1789, Camille Desmoulins jumped onto one of the tables in a café in Palais Royal and urged the mob to take up arms against the aristocracy. Unlike previous times when the revolution seemed to fail due to disagreements over the color of the revolution, this time the momentum moved forward.

A tour of the famous cafés of Paris offers a wonderful peak into how some of the exciting periods of history unraveled in this city. And if you ever need a respite from history, you are likely to find a Starbucks nearby (serving Arabica coffee, in case you are concerned). But before you start, you need some terminology. Like other Europeans, the French also sweetened their coffee with milk and cream, popularizing the *café au lait*, a drink that later spread around the world. The café au lait is served in a large cup, sometimes a bowl, and has a lot of steamed milk with some coffee. For more coffee taste, ask for a *café creme*, which has less milk than the café au lait and the milk is lightly foamed. The difference between café creme and a cappuccino is subtle; the latter will often be recognized in France by some chocolate or cinnamon powder sprinkled on top. If you want even less milk, order a *café noisette*, which is a pretty good approximation of a macchiato. Order by using the more common Italian drink terminology at your own risk: you may have to put up with condescending looks from the waiters.

A distinctive characteristic of Parisian cafés is that the tables outside are often arranged to enable the enjoyment of the street as a virtual theater. In some cafés, the price of the coffee seems to include the fine show. Another reason that coffee can be pretty pricey in Paris is the tendency of some clients to overstay their welcome. Jean-Paul Sartre, one of the leaders of existentialism, was purportedly able to stretch a cup of coffee for up to 12 hours. Many cafés that could not afford the likes of Sartre had to close down, decreasing the number of cafés significantly over the last 50 years.

Start the café tour of Paris at Café de la Paix on the right bank, just across the street from the Opera House. In the early coffee days of Paris, cafés were built along the grand boulevards of the city. Opened in 1872, Café de la Paix is the only one remaining from the Belle Époque. Designed by the same architect who built the Opera House itself, its interior is in the Belle Époque style with its gold accents and marble pillars. It is here that after the liberation of Paris from the Nazis, Charles de Gaulle ate an omelet just before taking his triumphal walk down to Champs-Elysées from the Étoile to the Place de la Concorde.

For a different genre of upscale experience, head to the cafés of St. Germain. As the Germans moved into Montparnasse in the late 1930's, Simone de Beauvoir and Jean-Paul Sartre, colleagues, lovers and leaders of existentialism, moved to the cafés of St. Germain which became the new center of Parisian intellectual life. This center revolved around what is now known as Place Sartre-Beauvoir, around which Café Deux Magot, Café de Flore and Brasserie Lipp are located.

The back room of Le Fumoir, a café just outside the Louvre Museum.

Les Deux Magot opened in 1875 and attracted quite a few notable patrons in its time. This was purportedly the meeting place of Verlaine, Ribaud, and Mallarme, three of the greatest French poets. Pablo Picasso and George Braque heralded the Cubist Movement into life here. During the last year leading up to his death, Oscar Wilde had his coffees here. The café gets its name from the two porcelain Chinese wise men that are mounted on the pillars inside.

Café de Flore had a special place in the hearts of Beauvoir and Sartre. Beauvoir referred to it as "*my home*" in her memoirs. Working upstairs at separate tables, even during air raids, she and Sartre made this café the headquarters of the Existentialist Movement. It was also the favorite place for meetings between Picasso and Chagall. In contrast, Brasserie Lipp, across the street from these two cafés, is known more for hosting politicians and has been frequented by every French president since Charles de Gaulle.

Today, one of the most vibrant café scenes is back in Montparnasse, where Anaïs Nin relished in her erotic fantasies. In addition to Le Coupole, one of the fixtures of this area is Café du Dome, which as of 1929 had already been mentioned in 50 books in 15 languages. Guillaume Apollinaire had summed up the Dome's inimitable role in the arts aptly: "*Here it is decided which French artists will be admired in Germany.*" Café Le Select, a subject of several scenes in Ernest Hemingway's *The Sun Also Rises,* is also one of the classics here. Sporting a vibrant art display, Le Select remains a favorite destination for French writers and artists and is well worth a visit.

Of course not all cafés in Paris have been around for over a century. There are many newcomers that are fun to visit and where you will actually see French people. These young cafés work hard to develop character to compete and survive in such a history-rich and lore-filled city. To clarify that they belong to a new genre, they will quickly point out that they serve 100% Arabica coffee beans. One such cafe that has particularly pleasing interiors is Le Fumoir (despite its name, smoking is not allowed there), across the street from the Louvre. The shelves in the back room are full of books that patrons can trade for their own, a custom

The square next to Le Deux Magots and café de Flore has been named after their colorful patrons.

in some Parisian cafés. Some of the other newer cafés try to distinguish themselves through modern designs, perhaps a retro look, or an audaciously expressive graffiti wall.

To the coffee connoisseur, Paris and the rest of France are not yet a dream destination. However, this land of enchanting cafés presents inviting opportunities for cafepreneurs. ✍

CAFÉ QUATRE GATS IN BARCELONA: Pre-Paris Picasso

PABLO PICASSO, ONE OF THE GREATEST ARTISTS OF THE 20TH CENTURY, was one of the more colorful patrons in many of the grand cafés of Paris. But his career started in Café Els Quatre Gats in Barcelona when at the age of 17 he gave his first public display in the café's back room in 1899. As a lasting token of appreciation and tribute, his beautiful art still graces the cover of the café's menu.

Café Quatre Gats opened in 1897 with great fanfare. The main founder was Pere Romeu, a cabaret waiter in Paris' Chat Noir who wanted to replicate some of the buoyant ambiance in Barcelona. He used to sit with his customers and chair debates about the world order. The large picture on the wall showing Romeu on a bicycle for two now enshrines him.

Café Quatre Gats was the meeting place of several celebrated artists who later became known as the "*Els Quatre gats group*" in Spanish art history. Other famous figures such as the architect Antoni Gaudi, musician Isaac Alberniz and his friends Enric Granados and Lluis Millet were also among the regular patrons.

The café closed down in 1903 and reopened only in the 1970s after extended restoration. The whimsical spirit of the place and its patron Picasso are well-preserved. From the tiled bar in the front room to the panoramic wall art, the café's decor is an evocative feast for the eyes. ✎

The back room of Café Quatre Gats where Picasso held his first exhibition (above) and the menu cover created by Picasso (right)

PRAGUE: Absinthe and Longing for Paris

FEW CAFÉS CAN CLAIM THE HONOR of being the subject of a poem written by a Nobel Laureate. *Café Slavie*, written by the Czech poet Jaroslav Seifert, beautifully captures not only the view and the mood of in the café, but also the deep fascination that the Czech intellectuals had with Paris and their love of their local beverage, the absinthe.

Café Slavia is not an ordinary café. It is the highlight of Prague's vibrant café scene. Founded in 1884, its location across the street from the national theater made it a favorite among the city's artists and intellectuals. The floor-to-ceiling windows offer views of the Vltava River, the Charles Bridge, and the Prague Castle. Because of its strategic location, the Slavia was a perfect vista point from which to witness some of the major events in Prague's history: the arrival of the Nazis, the invasion of Soviet tanks, and finally, as was carefully planned by Václav Havel at the Slavia itself, the marchers of the Velvet Revolution who overthrew communism. Ironically, after the liberation of Prague from the communists, the Slavia was closed for a few years due to a very capitalist-style real estate dispute. It re-opened in 1997 and was then restored to its 1930's glory with an art deco interior. The menu has an extensive selection of coffee-based beverages, and the display of cakes is strategically placed close to the entrance. If you ask at the front, they will also let you leaf through a book about the café that recounts the events and characters that have left indelible marks.

Characterized by vivacious art and intellectual rigor, Prague boasted one of the liveliest pre-World War II café cultures of Europe. Even though the post-war communist rule deemed some of the cafés too decadent and shut them down, the glory of some of the cafés has been restored for today's enjoyment. The delightful cafés you will encounter as you stroll around this beautiful city offer a welcome respite from its many attractions. For example, if you are climbing up to the Prague Palace on Zamecke Road, you will be hard-pressed to miss Café Neruda with its charming round tables covered by coffee-themed table cloth (which my wife and I expended significant effort to obtain for our house).

When visiting the Prague Cubist Museum, check out the Grand Orient Café on the second floor that has been written up in *The New York Times*. Fortunately, thanks to considerable Italian influence, the coffee you will taste at these places will be the best Prague has ever known.

Filling the same role as Jean-Paul Sartre in Paris and Sigmund Freud in Vienna, the Grand Patron of Prague cafés was the Prague-born Jewish writer Franz Kafka. He used to conduct discussions with friend and colleague Max Brod at Café Slavia and Café Montmartre. Many of the characters in his stories were inspired by individuals he observed in Prague cafés. Some say that his novels always

Café Slavie (1967)

Through the secret door from the riverbank,
which was made of such clear glass,
that it is nearly invisible,
and whose curtains
are smeared with rose oil,
sometimes Guillaume Apollinaire came.
He still had his head bandaged from the war.
He sat down with us
and read brutally beautiful poems,
which Karel Teige translated immediately.
To the poet's honor
we drank absinthe.
It is greener
than all that is green,
and when we looked up from the table out of the windows,
beneath the riverbank, the Seine was flowing.
Oh yes, the Seine!
Because at a distance, widely straddled
the Eiffel tower stood.
Once Nezval ran in wearing a black bowler.
At the time, we did not have any idea,
not even he knew,
that Apollinaire wore such a hat,
when he fell in love
with the beautiful Louise de Coligny-Châtillou,
whom he used to call Lou.

Café Slavia, and an English translation of the poem written about the café by Nobel Laureate Jaroslav Seifert (translation courtesy of Lenka Zelena).

Café Franz Kafka, near the Jewish Quarter

Café Louvre

leave you a bit jittery, as if you had just consumed one too many cups of coffee. Whether Kafka liked coffee and how he took his coffee are still subjects of conjecture and debate among his followers.

If Kafka did like coffee, then he certainly had quite a menu to choose from in his native Prague. Many cafés offer an extensive selection of coffee drinks, including the usual combinations of coffee, milk and chocolate, but with a strong emphasis on alcohol. You can pretty much have any alcoholic beverage mixed in with your coffee. In addition to Baileys, whiskey, cointreau, rum or even grappa, the favorite spirit in Prague is Bohemian-style absinthe. Unlike other versions of absinthe, the Bohemian style lacks the anise and fennel flavors. In their place, wormwood and high alcohol content reign supreme. Prague cafés are also an excellent place to grab a bite or pamper your sweet tooth with cake, even if you have just spent a few days in Vienna.

Café Louvre is among the historic Prague cafés that exemplifies Prague intellectuals' fascination with Paris, starting from their names. Founded in 1902, Café Louvre is on the second floor of a building on the main drag, Národní Street. It boasts an impressively illustrated staircase. A brochure details the history of the café and there are souvenirs for purchase. With its pink and cream walls, Neo-Rococo stucco moldings, and comfortable seating, the café is evocative of the Belle Époque. The café served Prague's high society before the communists closed it down in 1948. To the delight of the locals and tourists alike, it reopened in 1992.

Continuing with the French theme, Café Montmartre on Tetezova street

Café Neruda on the way up to the Prague Castle.

offers a much more intimate atmosphere. The café was better known as "cabaret montmarte." During World War I when France had become the enemy, the café was renamed to Montwaltner, after its owner Josef Waltner who was also an excellent dancer and lecturer. This was a favorite place for artists and writers where the evening programs were held in Czech, German and Yiddish, reflecting the cultural diversity of the city. The café also displayed various Cubist paintings. Jiri Kroha, a Czech architect and painter, arranged the entire room in a Cubist-Expressionist style and black masses were celebrated in front of a grand Cubist altar. A story tells that Waltner himself had even read from a missal while young girls in underwear served as altar servants. No one is sure whether these acts were meant to be artistic or purely for entertainment. Today, this café is a meeting place for the younger generation. I was fortunate to meet a group of university students, one of whom happily found and translated Seifert's poem about Café Slavia into English. ✑

BRATISLAVA: Rebirth of Coffee Culture

TUCKED AWAY ON ONE OF THE SIDE STREETS of Old Town Bratislava is Café Malevil. The café's inner courtyard beckons passers by to sit all afternoon and sink into deep thought. The interior of the café, with its arched ceiling and imaginative decor, transports your mind into an ethereal state. After negotiating an off-the-menu macchiato, I asked the barista about the origin of the café's name. She explained that the owner was a fan of the 1981 movie *Malevil*, based on a post-apocalyptic novel by the French writer Robert Merle. The novel tells of one Emanuel Compte, a respected farmer and former school director who runs a castle as a tourist attraction in rural France. One day, Emanuel and a few of his friends found them-

Café Malevil, one of the most charming cafés in Bratislava

selves in the wine cellar of the castle and heard some loud noises. When they came out of the cellar, they realized that an unexpected nuclear war had just flattened the entire country to ashes. They started to wander around, found additional survivors, and resuscitated life from the ashes.

After strolling through Old Town Bratislava for a few hours, the story of Café Malevil took on a new layer of meaning as a metaphor for the city's café culture, a metaphor that also applies to other parts of Eastern Europe where café culture is starting to blossom again. Bratislava, also known under a few other names such as Pressburg (mostly by Germans) and Pozsony (mostly by Hungarians), has a long and rich history. It had been a multicultural city that enjoyed Austrian, Hungarian, German, Slovak, Czech and Jewish influences. At one point Bratislava was the capital of the Kingdom of Hungary and the seat of regal coronations. In the middle of the 18th century, Bratislava flourished especially during the reign of the Austrian Empress Maria Theresia who also had a hand in the flourishing of Trieste, an Italian coffee mecca. In short, coffee culture was invigorating and cafés were the center of social and intellectual life in Bratislava beginning in the 18th century, and peaking during the 19th century.

After the communists seized control of Czechoslovakia in 1948, the cafés and related coffee culture vanished. Even as recently as ten years ago, it was a challenge to find a good cup of coffee in Bratislava. The Communist Party of Czechoslovakia was overthrown in 1989 in the "Velvet Revolution" (known for the lack of violence involved). After the 1993 "Velvet Divorce" from the Czech Republic, Bratislava became the capital of the independent Republic of Slovakia. At that turning point, coffee culture was reborn. Café Malevil is one of many young cafés budding around the city, recreating the invigorating atmosphere the city once knew.

Another café with a distinct Slovakian touch is Café U Certa, located on the way from the town center to the Bratislava Castle. In Slovak, *U Certa* means 'the devil.' With skeletons hanging on the wall and their arms and feet protruding from the ceiling, the decor of the café makes good on the imagery. Here you can also witness how cafés in this part of Europe blur the boundaries between the café and the pub. On a warm day in August, most of the patrons were ordering beer, not cappuccino.

Cafés line the streets of Old Town and beyond. The Coffee&Co chain, which could be seen as the Slovakian version of Starbucks, seems to dominate. Bratislavians appreciate good coffee and are willing to pay extra for a good and nicely served cup. The city even has an annual coffee competition among the local cafés that is aimed at raising awareness for good coffee (and of course, some subliminal marketing). Whatever they drink, Bratislava offers a beguiling atmosphere for long hours of people watching. ✍

ITALY: Passion for Coffee

NO PLACE COMES TO MIND MORE READILY THAN ITALY when you think of passion for coffee par excellence. Anywhere in the world, a café that advertises "Italian coffee" is trying to capitalize on that quintessential reputation. While bad coffee may be found anywhere, you are likely to find fine coffee virtually everywhere in Italy. This is a country in which Starbucks did not even *try* to open a store. Italy has the largest number of coffee bars per capita with approximately 100,000 in a country of about 60 million people. To put that in perspective, Starbucks has less than 20,000 stores worldwide.

Speaking of "the" coffee culture in Italy would be overly simplistic. Italy is composed of a rich tapestry of local coffee cultures that vary quite drastically from place to place. The south favors rather short and very strong espresso that matches well with the more piquant flavors of the local foods (and the prevalent lactose intolerance). In the north, more milk is present in the coffee drinks. Northern Italian roast is typically lighter than the roast found in the south. In Venice, a macchiatone (what some consider to be the perfect combination of milk and espresso) may be ordered in any café. If you stray from the Venice-Verona region, the chances that people will recognize the concept of a macchiatone greatly diminish. In Milano, a marocchino is a somewhat similar drink. In Naples, the macchiatone has been dismissed as *"another American invention."* Ordering a caffe sospeso (literally a coffee "in suspense") as a sign of your good fortune is a distinctively Neapolitan tradition. The customer pays for two coffees when ordering a sospeso, but only receives one. That way, when a person who is having a bad day or otherwise down on his luck comes into the café, he may ask if there are any coffees held in suspense and become the beneficiary of the first customer's generosity. Be prepared for an additional jolt to your senses in Torino, where the art of fusing chocolate and espresso has been perfected in a sublime drink known as the *bicerin*.

Caffè Quadri, on Piazza San Marco in Venice.

The earliest evidence of Turkish merchants bringing coffee to Italy comes from an unlikely source. Police records from 1575 show that among the belongings of the murdered Turkish merchant Huseyin Celebi was his *finian*, the pot used to make Turkish coffee. At the time, Venice was an independent and very powerful city-state that controlled the maritime trade routes to the Ottoman Empire and the Far East. Coffee used to travel from the port of Mocha in Yemen, through the port of Alexandria, and then to Venice. Venice was responsible for importing much of the coffee into Europe and opening some of the early coffeehouses.

Caffè Florian, across the piazza from Caffè Quadri.

Originally, coffee met with some resistance in Venice as the church did not want cafés to grow and become forums of open exchange. The Venetian State even sent spies to the cafés to ensure that the conversations did not stray. Cafés were limited to only small rooms that allowed four to six people to congregate in not too comfortable environs so the gathering would not be unduly long. In fact, Caffè Florian, the oldest and still active Venetian café on the Piazza San Marco, started out in this form. The café opened in 1720 under the name Venezia Triofante (Venice Triumphant), a bit ironic given Venice's declining status at the time. It was later renamed after its founder.

In 1775, Giorgio Quadri from Corfu founded Caffè Quadri across the piazza from Caffè Florian, instigating an interesting rivalry that continues until today. In the beginning, Caffè Quadri's claim to fame involved permitting gambling and renting rooms for '*purposes of debauch.*' Both cafés are known for having entertaining orchestras that sometimes performed in competition and at other times in tandem. The contrast between the two cafés was most pronounced during the Austrian occupation of Venice: the Austrians chose the Quadri, while the locals remained faithful to the Florian. Some have noted that the Florian was the place where everyone congregated, no matter their nationality. Both cafés attracted an impressive list of patrons over the years, often sharing them on a daily basis. Henry James used to breakfast at the Florian and lunch at the Quadri. By the mid 1800's, the entire Piazza San Marco had become lined with cafés, each sporting a large terrace for its patrons to enjoy the sun and the mesmerizing views. However, the Florian and the Quadri remain the must-visit landmarks today.

The most significant contribution of Italy to world coffee culture is no doubt the espresso that has revolutionized café culture on a global scale and was enabled by the sophisticated machinery that the Italians refined over the years. Like many other things in Italy, the espresso arose from the desire to combine influences from the East and the West. From the East, the espresso borrows the Turkish convention of a strong cup of coffee served in a demitasse. From the West, the espresso adopts the Viennese influence of filtering the coffee and adding milk. Once the fusion was conceived, a technological race began to produce the best espresso machines.

The word espresso derives from the Italian word for fast. A cup of coffee needs to be prepared very quickly in order to serve many customers. Two more layers of equally applicable interpretations are: every espresso cup is prepared expressly for the customer in the specific fashion that the customer prefers; and the way in which espresso is prepared extracts the best aspects of the coffee, thereby expressing the coffee at its most exquisite.

Unlike cafés in other parts of the world, the Italian coffee bar was not designed for drawn out socialization or contemplation. As University of Trento professor Yannis Velegrakis aptly summarized, "*in Italy, coffee is a short and intense emotion.*" Most of the socialization at the Italian coffee bar is designed to be brief and typically to be carried out standing around the bar. Of course, you are always welcome to sit down and contribute to the café's rent by paying four or five times more for the same drink. A cappuccino could easily cost you seven Euros at a Venetian café, whereas the price of coffee when standing at the bar is governed by local laws and typically around one Euro. There are other reasons for this attribute of Italian coffee bars. One is that socialization is meant to occur several times a day. So each one ends up being rather short. For example, you may meet a friend at a bar at 8am and then again at 11am, perhaps come back briefly after lunch at 1pm, and then later in the afternoon, or before going home. Another reason is that traditionally, Italy was not a very rich country where people had the means to sit in opulent cafés as they did in Paris or Vienna. Most of the 100,000 coffee bars in Italy are run on very small margins by a couple with very little assistance. Sales of pastries, panini, and of course, alcohol, help supplement the low margins from coffee.

The Bialetti coffee pot is another time-honored Italian classic found in many Italian homes. The 8-sided design is over 70 years old and has been common in Italian kitchens since the 1950s. The pot is named after the engineer who perfected the Mocha Express, the coffee pot that is credited with making coffee accessible to a wider spectrum of the population. The pot is designed to allow boiling water percolate through coffee grounds, producing a tasty cup of coffee. Today, with the increased availability of capsule-based espresso machines such as the Nespresso, Italians are drinking more of their coffee at home, leading to a steady decline in visits to coffee bars.

TRIESTE: The Anti-Venice

NO OTHER CITY IN ITALY REPRESENTS THE ITALIAN SPIRIT OF COFFEE better than Trieste. Located in the northeast corner of the Adriatic Sea a few minutes drive from the border with Slovenia, Trieste is a port town of about 200,000 people that sits at the crossroads of multiple cultures. The story of Trieste came to life most poignantly when Vinko Sandalj, the past president of the Trieste Coffee Association, described his uncle's life: "*He lived all of his life in the exact same house in the Trieste area, but had six nationalities—Austro-Hungarian, Italian, German Occupation (Adriatisches Küstenland during WW-II), the Free Territory of Trieste, Yugoslavian and Croatian.*" The city is also known for being the birthplace of Illy Caffe, arguably the best-known Italian coffee label. Even though Trieste is past its peak, it is still responsible for 30% of the coffee that moves through Italy and for 10% of the country's coffee processing. Trieste is home to over 50 coffee-related organizations, ranging the full industry gamut from warehouse owners, importers, traders and roasters,

Caffè San Marco in Trieste

Nestled up on a hill overlooking Trieste is a greenhouse full of coffee plants. In the mid-1990's, Ernesto Illy asked Giorgio Graziosi, a biology professor at the university, what is known about the genetics of coffee. Professor Graziosi's literature survey revealed what every researcher dreams to find: very little prior work. Illy then provided Graziosi generous funding with which Graziosi has created the biggest genetic database of coffee that is available to anyone on the Web.

to a few landmark cafés and even a coffee university.

The history of Trieste is marked by a few unsuccessful wars against its powerful neighbor Venice, after which Trieste sought protection from Austria in the 14th century. In the 18th century, Trieste received the status of a "free port city" and began to flourish during the reign of Empress Maria Theresia. This special status not only gave Trieste autonomy to handle its own taxes, but more importantly, provided religious freedom. People from a multitude of backgrounds and cultures flowed into the city, resulting in a bustling and cosmopolitan center. To this day, Trieste is the only major Italian city that does not have a *duomo* as the cornerstone of its main piazza. In fact, the city houses the second largest synagogue in Europe. When I first met Vinko, he thought I was writing a book about the Jewish role in the coffee world and underscored the significant Jewish influence on the coffee trade in Trieste. Coincidentally, many of the Jews were from Thessaloniki, Greece, the hometown of the paternal side of my family for centuries.

Vinko Sandalj is a fountain of knowledge concerning coffee in Italy and beyond. In addition to heading the local coffee organization and mentoring coffee professionals throughout Italy, he is one of the founders of the European Specialty Coffee Association and a past member of the Board of Directors of the Cup of Excellence, the organization that runs the farmer competitions known as the "Oscars of Coffee." Vinko took over the management of the Sandalj Coffee trading company from his father some years ago. His true passion for coffee blossomed as he was touring the coffee growing regions of the world researching his own coffee book *Coffee: A Celebration of Diversity*.

A visit to Vinko's spacious office is akin to a trip to a small coffee museum. Enviably situated on the canal-lined street in the center of Trieste, it is adorned with various coffee memorabilia including train-shaped antique coffee machines, hand grinders and other coffee collectibles. In addition to importing coffee from all over the world and selling them to roasters, Sandalj Coffee also creates blends of beans for specific customer profiles. Some of the coffee taste preferences that have emerged over the years for historical and supply reasons persist today even if the original reasons are no longer relevant. For example, Sandalj would not sell a blend that contains 100% Arabica beans to customers in Sicily because it simply would not appeal to their palate. Sandalj's Taster-in-Chief Edy Bieker is always busy designing blends that satisfy the different preferences and eager to share his creations with every visitor.

TORINO: Espresso and Chocolate in Perfect Matrimony

THE HISTORIES OF COFFEE AND CHOCOLATE ARE CLOSELY INTERTWINED even though their geographical trajectories are mirror images of each other. Coffee originated in Africa and migrated to South and Central America where most of the world's coffee is currently grown. Cocoa, on the other hand, originated in Mexico and Central America and migrated to Africa where the Ivory Coast and Ghana currently produce most of the world's supply.

With the incredible culinary potential of both of these beans, the fusion of chocolate and coffee has been investigated and experimented by many. Nowhere has this quest been taken as seriously and artfully as in Torino. As my wife says, "*One would be hard pressed to find a more romantic coffee search destination to seduce a chocoholic lover than Torino.*"

Located in the northwestern corner of Italy bordering France, Torino has a long tradition of chocolate innovations. Its streets are lined with chocolatiers displaying tantalizing arrays of delectable chocolate confections. This is the birthplace of gianduja, that irresistible concoction of hazelnut and chocolate. Gianduja is a key ingredient in Nutella, which is sold in over 75 countries.

Enchantingly seduced by a bicerin

The streets of Torino city center are endowed with a remarkable concentration of magnificent cafés. Some of these, such as the Fiorio and the Baratti e Milano, have a rich history dating back over 200 years.

The drink that distinguishes Torino's cafés from all others is the *bicerin*. The bicerin was named after the particular type of transparent glass in which it was first served. While the cafés offer different versions of the bicerin, the compulsory stop is Caffè Al Bicerin where the original (and secretly guarded) recipe still entices and captivates on a daily basis.

Founded in 1763, Caffè Al Bicerin sits in a quaint piazza across from one of Torino's landmarks, the Santuario of the Consolata. It is an intimate and well-preserved architectural treasure that is embellished by elegant 18th century decor of wooden panels, marble table tops, and an old-fashioned counter behind which a colorful display of gianduja-based sweets beckon. The founders of

Animated barista shows are included in the price of the bicerin (pictured below).

the café had dabbled with a few drinks that combined chocolate and coffee. There was the *pur-e-fior* (espresso and cream, closest to today's cappuccino), *pur-e-barba* (espresso and chocolate) and finally, they hit a home run with the *un po 'd tu*t (espresso, Gianduja and cream).

Because the drink was adored by the nobility and the common folk alike, Caffè Al Bicerin became a place where multiple social classes rubbed shoulders freely. That the bicerin was allowed during periods of religious fasting (because hot chocolate was not considered food) further enhanced its popularity, especially after mass at the Santuario. Famous café patrons have included Dumas, Puccini, Nietzsche, and Cavour, the statesman who is credited with reuniting Italy.

The multiple layers of the heavenly bicerin have inspired many superlative descriptions, including "*a feat of culinary engineering*" and "*an alliance of perfect proportions.*" When we finally sat down to experience this uniquely Torinese ritual, the elixir exceeded our expectations: "*espresso and chocolate in perfect matrimony*" proclaimed my wife. Even an hour after the last sip, the heady combination of sensuous cream, velvety espresso, and ambrosial gianduja continued to linger. To experience this exceptionally luscious seduction dating back more than two centuries is well worth a special trip to Torino! ❧

GERMANY, SWITZERLAND AND THE NETHERLANDS:
Europe's Big Coffee Businesses

A GOOGLE SEARCH FOR "SWITZERLAND COFFEE CULTURE" yields as its first result a YouTube video showing Roger Federer the famed tennis player extolling the virtues of an automatic espresso machine made by the Swiss company Jura. Dressed dapperly and perched on a couch, Federer shares that it was a *"dream come true"* for him when Jura approached him to be their ambassador. He had just bought a Jura espresso machine and could not say enough good things about it.

This anecdote is emblematic not only of Switzerland's contribution to coffee culture, but also of Germany's and the Netherlands'. The three countries can be credited mostly in connection with their contributions to the coffee business. The Swiss flooded the world with coarse instant coffee and are trying to redeem themselves with the more refined Nespresso. The Dutch succeeded in smuggling a coffee plant from Yemen in 1615 and became the world's major coffee trader in the 17th century. As Europe's largest coffee importer, the Germans humored us with their rulers' failed attempts to keep beer as their national drink and gifted us with the Bach *Coffee Cantata*.

Federer's endorsement aside, the Swiss are renowned for skillfully marrying superior technology and elegant design. Though they did not invent instant coffee (that was done initially by a Japanese American chemist, Satori Kato, and a few years later an American named George Constant Louis Washington figured out a process for mass producing it), they did invent Nescafé, which is synonymous with instant coffee in most parts of the world. Today, Nestle is impacting the coffee market in a more positive way with its sleek Nespresso line of home espresso machines that are catching on quickly. Attractive Nespresso boutique stores display innovative designs of their polychromatic trademark capsules. The coffees produced from the rainbow array of capsules are often better than those found in many local cafés. And if you actually live in expensive Switzerland, the spiffy machine and accompanying capsules will save you an arm and a leg.

In his novel, *The Coffee Trader*, David Liss vividly depicts the trading scene in Amsterdam as coffee came onto the stage. Amsterdam was a bustling trading hub in the 17th century. Unfortunately, coffee at the time was so closely guarded by the Yemenites that only roasted or otherwise sterile beans were let out of the ports of Yemen. As the worldwide demand for coffee grew, the need for additional sources of the bean arose. Around 1615, the Dutch leveraged their dominant position in the world maritime supply routes to smuggle a coffee plant onto a ship from Aden, Yemen to Amsterdam and kept it in a greenhouse. In 1714, the Dutch gifted Louis XIV a progeny of the original

Café Hoppe: the oldest café in Amsterdam

plant. In 1723, that gift embarked on coffee's most dramatic voyage, from Paris to Martinique, during which army Captain Gabriel de Clieu heroically guarded the coffee plant so he could bring it to the New World.

A few decades after the original plant made its way from Yemen to Amsterdam, the Dutch spread coffee beans across their territories and began cultivating coffee in Ceylon (now Sri Lanka), Java, Sumatra, Celebes and Timor in the East Indies, and Dutch Guyana in the West Indies, not too far from where de Clieu had ended his trip across the Atlantic. The coffee brought to Dutch Guyana was recently discovered to be of a different varietal than the beans brought by de Clieu, establishing two independent sources to what is now the largest coffee growing region in the world. At the time, the Dutch became so powerful with their new sources of coffee that they were able to actually set the prices of coffee on the world market.

The most notable Dutch tradition related to coffee (which according to a recent poll, 75% of Dutch people want to preserve) is the cookie or biscuit that goes with it. The biscuit is often served from a tin, but you may only reach for it when the hostess offers one. The number of cookies has often been interpreted as an additional social signal: one cookie a sign of stinginess, three of warm hospitality. These treats are served in any of Amsterdam's hodgepodge of cafés, from the Café Hoppe that dates back to 1670, the elegant Café Americain with its well-preserved Art Deco interior, to the city's famed hash cafés where the menus offer a selection of drugs in addition to coffee.

Though it is still challenging to find a great cup of coffee in Amsterdam today, the specialty coffee industry is starting to take off. According to Liesbeth Sleijster and Rose Van Asten, both former Dutch barista champions who run the coffee consulting and training firm Cocoon Coffee, coffee quality and expert preparation are receiving increased attention. With specialty roasters such as Boot Koffie and Trabocca, great coffee is now served in Amsterdam cafés such as Espressofabriek, Screaming Beans and the family-run Coffee To Walk.

The interior of Café Americain, one of the city's landmark historic cafés

As the largest coffee market in Europe, Germany imports more than twice as much coffee as any other country on the continent. Germany also exports more coffee than any other country in Europe, meaning that quite a few folks in Europe are buying beans roasted in Germany. Coffeehouses started spreading through Germany in the 1670's, giving birth to *kaffeklatsch*, the concept of coffee plus gossip, typically for elderly women. In 1777, Frederick the Great decided that the drink had become too popular, or more precisely, that he could no longer stand all the café gossip about him. He began to clamp down by restricting the roasting and sale of coffee in the country. Much to his chagrin, the German women were particularly enamored of their new socialization venues and were vocal in resisting his tight controls. While his attempts to restrict coffee ultimately failed, the whole affair endowed the world with one of Frederick's most memorable quotes: *"It is disgusting to note the increase in the quantity of coffee used by my subjects and the amount of money that goes out of the country in consequence. Everybody is using coffee. If possible, this must be prevented. My people must drink beer."*

The great German composer Johann Sabastian Bach made a lasting contribution to coffee culture in the form of his *Coffee Cantata*. It is a secular cantata (essentially a miniature comic opera) written by Bach between 1732 and 1734. The *Coffee Cantata* is a comedic showdown between a father and his daughter Lieschen. This satirical commentary amusingly depicts Lieschen's addiction to coffee and entertainingly reveals the resulting intergenerational conflicts, two pressing social problems in 18th century Germany. When the father urged Leischen to stop drinking coffee, Leischen replied in exactly the way many of us feel every morning:

Café Odeon in Zurich.

Father, don't be so severe!
If I can't drink
my bowl of coffee three times daily,
then in my torment I will shrivel up
like a piece of roast goat.

The two go on sparring with each other for a while, until the father pulls out his main card:

Well then, you'll have to resign yourself
to never taking a husband.

Leischen takes this threat more seriously, and she avers that coffee will remain forever untouched. But while her father is out searching for a worthy mate, Leischen pursues Plan B:

but Leischen secretly lets it be known:
no suitor is to come to my house
unless he promises me,
and it is also written into the marriage contract,
that I will be permitted
to make myself coffee whenever I want.

The social controversies eventually fizzled out. By the time Ludwig van Beethoven was born some 20 years after Bach's death, coffee drinking had become much better accepted in Germany. Interestingly, Beethoven' claim to fame in the world of coffee was his fastidiousness about using exactly 60 beans when he made his cup of coffee.

Today, Germany exports a unique kind of coffee experience called Tchibo. Established in 1949 and competing against Germany's other big roaster, Jacobs Kaffee, Tchibo realized after some time that margins from coffee sales were insufficient to keep up with growth. They then expanded product offerings to include women's lingerie and other household goods in addition to coffee. Now that's a scintillating kaffeklatsch if ever there was one! ✑

Oriana Halevy modelling coffee & lingerie at a Tchibo store in Vienna.

BOSNIA: Coffee in Happiness and in Sorrow

ON JULY 11TH, 2004, THE NINTH ANNIVERSARY of the gruesome 1995 Srebrenica genocide, Aida Sehović created an installation in front of a mosque in Sarajevo to commemorate the 7,000–10,000 men and boys who lost their lives in the massacre. Aida laid 939 cups of coffee that she collected from the community on a 30-meter patch of soil in the shape of Bosnia and Herzegovina. She brewed coffee on location and slowly poured it into the cups. In some of the cups she only put a cube of sugar, in memory of the children who were killed in the massacre and were too young to drink coffee. The installation was called *"sto te nema?"* ("why are you not here?"). As Aida explains, sharing a cup of coffee in Bosnian culture is a deep-rooted ritual and longing to share a cup of coffee with the deceased is an intimate expression of sorrow.

A man participating in Aida Sehović's installation by pouring coffee into the cups.

I was first tipped off to the distinctive Bosnian coffee culture when a Croatian waiter at Café Central in Vienna animatedly described an encounter he had in a café in Sarajevo. After gulping down his coffee, he had gotten up to ask for the bill. He was quite shocked to hear the following retort: *"Mister, I will pay for your coffee, but please never come to my café again."* When he inquired what he had done wrong, the waiter explained that in Bosnia you simply do not rush through your coffee and go. Tradition and custom dictate that people linger for a few hours sipping coffee. Anything less is an insult.

I decided that I must experience Bosnian coffee culture firsthand. I was fortunate to be introduced through my Facebook network to Lejla Djuric, a Bosnian law student from Tuzla and her twin brother Zeljko, a web developer. They graciously spent a few days taking me around Sarajevo and gave me a primer on Bosnian politics and culture.

Known to be a moderate city that accepts religious diversity, Sarajevo has earned the nickname "Little Jerusalem." The heart of Sarajevo is its old town, with narrow cobble-

A small pot filled with coffee, a cup and a small bowl for sugar or *rahatluk*, a Bosnian sweet

stone alleys that are lined with shops. In a matter of minutes you can wander by a mosque, a cathedral, a church, and a synagogue. The influence of the Austro-Hungarian rule on Sarajevo becomes palpable just minutes away from the old city where the boulevards are wide and lined with stately buildings that make you wonder if you have just arrived in Vienna. As may be expected, the politics here are very complicated. The Dayton Agreement that brought an end to the war in 1995 had to spell out a complex arrangement in which the country is governed by three presidents. It takes quite a bit of lingering over coffee to fully appreciate all the issues here.

Coffee culture is ingrained in the Bosnian consciousness. Bosnians would say that coffee is an integral part of their identity and the basis of their social fabric. You never prepare coffee only for yourself: even if you are alone at home, you will always prepare enough coffee for another person just in case a friend drops by. And when someone does come by, there are different words to refer to the coffee, depending on when it is served. Upon arrival, the first coffee is called "*docekusa*" (derived from the verb *docekati* which means to welcome). The "*razgovorusa*" (derived from the word *razgovor* meaning "conversation") is the coffee consumed as the visit proceeds. Upon parting, the "goodbye" coffee is called "*sikterusa*," though you need to be careful with that word because in Turkey it has negative connotations.

Visitors may have any number of espresso drinks in Sarajevo, but that would be missing the point. To experience true Bosnian café culture, go into one of the traditional cafés in the old town, such as Café Dibek, Male Daire or Café Sevdah. As you enter, you will find yourself slipping back 400 years in time into a café you would have expected to see in Istanbul in the 16th century, except now there is free wireless. Bosnian coffee is served on a round tray that includes a *dzezva*, the coffee pot, and a *fildzan*, the small cup. On the side there will be a small sugar bowl with a cube of sugar and a *rahatluk*, a typical Bosnian sweet. If you request, you will also receive a hookah and a clean mouthpiece so you can smoke the filtered fruity tobacco. The scene here is very relaxed. Young people will hang out for hours, enjoying each other's company, smoking the hookah, and discussing the latest and hippest happenings of the day. If the coffee needs to be kept warm for a long while, a mangala will be provided. No one is in any hurry at these venues.

To the uninformed, Bosnian coffee may seem much like Turkish coffee. However, there are important differences that change the taste considerably. Unlike the Turks who boil the water directly with the coffee grounds, the Bosnians first boil the water, then add the coffee grounds and bring the mixture back to a boil. Besides, as the Bosnians note, the Turks drink mostly tea.

Bosnians will try to resolve any conflict over coffee. For example, if you get into a car accident, both parties will go for a cup of coffee and discuss how to settle the damages. Drinking coffee together is a common way for university students to build and solidify relationships.

The scene inside Male Daire, where hookahs are provided with the coffee.

It is perfectly acceptable for a poor student to take his girlfriend out to coffee instead of a fancy restaurant because it is more meaningful to take her to a quiet place to have a conversation. Fortunately, social norms in this coffee-dominated culture do permit you to skip the coffee ritual when you bring your girlfriend back to your apartment. There is no point in wasting good beans.

I gained further appreciation of the Bosnian coffee culture by spending some time (over coffee, of course) with Vedad Brkanic, in his shop in the Old Town of Sarajevo. The shelves of Vedad's shop are stacked with coffee pots, cups and manual grinders, as well as other copper accessories that have been made by his family for the past 270 years. Vedad confided that sharing a coffee is an expression of enduring friendship and hospitality which he may indulge in ten to twelve times a day. Yet no matter how caffeinated he becomes, he still enjoys a cup of coffee with his wife in the evening when he gets home. If not, she will know something is wrong. Vedad puts it more romantically: "*I start my day with my wife and coffee and end my day with my wife and coffee.*"

A few stores down from Vedad we visit Jabucar H. Nasir (the middle initial signifies that Jabucar has gone to Mecca for the Hajj). Jabucar is the ninth generation artisan of a family that has been in Sarajevo for over 500 years. In addition to his business, Jabucar runs a workshop for training students in the art of pot-making. In 2004, he was commissioned to build the world's largest coffee pot. As he showed me the certificate he received from the Guinness World Records, he

Coffee pots on display in a Sarajevo shop.

Lejla and Zeljko Djurik and Vedad Brkanic in his shop in the Old Town of Sarajevo.

explained that it took him and his five students two and a half months to build a coffee pot that stands 124 centimeters tall and measures 95 centimeters in diameter. The pot has a capacity of 800 liters. If you add a mere 60 kilos of coffee you can fill 12,000 cups (*fildzans*) of coffee from the pot. But don't expect quick service—it takes two and a half hours to boil the water, and another half hour before the coffee grounds settle. Two months after my visit to Jabucar's shop, my wife and I were the only visitors to the Shanghai World Expo who went there expressly to snap a shot of the award-winning pot on exhibit at the Bosnian Pavilion. Alas, we arrived a couple of weeks too late, as the national treasure had already returned home.

After spending a few days in Bosnia, the profound meaning of Aida's installation started to sink in. Since the 2004 inaugural memorial, Aida has held the installation several times, always on the anniversary of the Srebrenica massacre, in cities such as New York (in front of the UN building), Stockholm, and Tuzla. The last installation grew to include over 3,000 cups. Over the years, the installation has transformed from being Aida's own project to being a perpetual living memorial, representing the collective experience of the participants who bring their own *fildzans*, place them anywhere they like with no preconceived layout, and pour the coffee themselves at whatever pace suits them. Through the kaleidoscopic array of cups and the coffee poured into them by diverse participants, the annual installations have come to symbolize not only bereavement and loss, but also reflective celebrations of the inseparable bonds connecting all Bosnians.

The street scene near
Café Male Daire

LONDON: Revival of the Oldest European Café Culture

AFTER A NEARLY THREE-CENTURY HIATUS (excluding a brief period of glory in the 1950's), London is back in a leadership position on the world coffee scene. Until the major clash of 1674, London had a pioneering coffee culture.

Coffeehouse-induced sexual tensions reached feverish levels in London when its women presented the "Women's Petition Against Coffee" to the King in 1674. The women started their protest in a relatively conciliatory tone, setting the background and restating the main reason to live in England:

> That since 'tis Reckon'd amongst the Glories of our Native Country, To be a Paradise for Women: The fame in our Apprehensions can consist in nothing more than the brisk Activity of our men, who in former Ages were justly esteemed the Ablest Performers in Christendome;

But then they wasted no time in getting to the point:

> But to our unspeakable Grief, we find of late a very sensible Decay of that true Old English Vigor; our Gallants being every way so Frenchified, that they are become meer Cock-sparrows, fluttering things that come on Sa sa, with a world of Fury, but are not able to stand to it, and in the very first Charge fall down flat before us.

and more specifically

> They come from it with nothing moist but their snotty Noses, nothing stiffe but their Joints, nor standing but their Ears.

Then, they identify the culprit:

Kaffeine, one of the newer cafés in London that was named best coffeehouse in Europe in 2010.

> after a furious Enquiry, and Discussion of the Point by the Learned of the Faculty, we can Attribute to nothing more than the Excessive use of that Newfangled, Abominable, Heathenish Liquor called COFFEE, which Riffling Nature of her Choicest Treasures, and Drying up the Radical Moisture, has so Eunucht our Husbands, and Cripple our more kind Gallants, that they are become as Impotent as Age, and as unfruitful as those Desarts whence that unhappy Berry is said to be brought.

The conclusion of the petition is a loud and clear demand that London coffeehouses be banned.

The background for the petition sheds some light on London's early coffee culture in the 17th century. Though a coffeehouse culture was thriving, it mostly catered to men's socialization needs. Some cafés offered "extra services" that the men were able to enjoy after

The first coffeehouse in England

drinking coffee. Despite being the '*ablest performers in Christendome*,' receiving these services had the effect of reducing their libido when they returned home.

Unfazed by the women's grievances, the Englishmen did not give up easily. Their response came swiftly, and began from the point of general agreement:

have we not condiscended to all the Methods of Debauchery? Invented more Postures than Aretine ever Dreamed of!

They then turned to defending their new paramour:

But why must innocent COFFEE be the object of your Spleen? That harmless and healing Liquor, which Indulgent Providence first sent amongst us, at a time when Brimmers of Rebellion, and Fanatick Zeal had intoxicated the Nation, and we wanted a Drink at once to make us Sober and Merry.

And the men even tried to convince the women that their increased free time is to their advantage:

Chat of there, you will not think it Impertinent, when you consider the fair opportunities you have thereby, of entertaining an obliging friend in our Absence.

And finally, offering the best on point defense they could concoct:

Coffee is the general Drink throughout Turky, and those Eastern Regions, and yet no part of the world can boast more able or eager performers, than those Circumcised Gentlemen, who, (like our modern Gallants) own no other joys of Heaven, than what consists in Veneral Titillations;

Though the Petition did not succeed in banning coffeehouses, the men ultimately lost this battle. By 1730, most of the coffeehouses had closed down and were replaced by the much more women-receptive tearooms. Because the coffee that the English enjoyed up to that point was never really any good, coffee lost its appeal as tea became more sophisticated and gained ascendancy. Having never owned any

Flat white, one of the new cafés in the Soho District.

coffee-growing colonies, the British had little financial incentive to continue importing the bean.

Opinions are divided on who introduced coffeehouses to England. Some attribute this to a Jew named Jacob who opened a coffeehouse in Oxford in 1650. Others give credit to a Greek gentleman named Pasqua Rosee who opened a coffeehouse in London in 1652. Rosee has garnered greater attention because his story is more interesting. Jacob's consolation prize is a plaque at the Grand Café in Oxford, the site of his original café.

When Pasqua Rosee lived in the ancient Turkish city of Smyrna (Izmir today), he was employed as a personal assistant to Daniel Edwards, an English merchant for the Levant Company. During his sojourn in Smyrna, Edwards and his father-in-law were exposed to the rich Turkish traditions surrounding coffee. They wanted to recreate some of the exotic experience upon returning to London. Since they were "*too grand and busy*" to open a coffeehouse, they sponsored Rosee to rise to the occasion. The decision to locate Rosee's Café on St. Michael's Alley, a narrow alley in Cornhill leading to the Royal Exchange, was driven by the hope that the merchants who congregated at the exchange every day would be willing to try out a drink that was "*as thick as puddle water*" and tasted like "*boiled soot.*"

Rosee's foreign accent and poor English added to his charm and helped sustain a brand name that was kept even after Rosee left the business. He was also recognized with a plaque. In 1952, the Corporation of London unveiled a blue plaque on the walls of the Jamaica Wine House, built on the original location of Rosee's first coffee shed. Today, Rosee's name lives on far beyond London, with Rosee cafés found as far as New Zealand and Egypt.

By 1700, there were over 2,000 cafés in London. Two features of these cafés helped foster very different social interactions than previously possible. First, unlike the tavern patrons, the café patrons were sober, alert, and often even articulate. Second, cafés offered an egalitarian meeting place where you may sit next to anyone, regardless of class or position in society. As the poet Samuel Butler put it, the coffeehouse "*admits of no distinction of persons, but gentleman, mechanic, lord and scoundrel mix, and all are of a piece, as if they were resolv'd into their first principles.*" Coffeehouses thus acted as class-levelers that afforded lively discussion. Coffeehouses were affectionately called "penny universities" because they provided the opportunity to learn many topics over penny-a-cup coffees. In 1675, King Charles II became disenchanted with the unrestricted freedom of discussions that flowed from such "publick intercourse" and sought to outlaw coffeehouses. However, dramatic outcry forced him to withdraw the ban two days before it was to take effect.

The plethora of coffeehouses in London included ones dedicated to special interests. For example, Isaac Newton frequented the Grecian Coffeehouse that was a venue for arts and sciences. For the literary types such as Jonathan Swift and Alexander Pope, there was Will's café. Painters such as Hogarth went to Old Slaughter's. There were coffeehouses for individual religions, political parties, clergy and trade as well. Interestingly, these special interest coffeehouses gave birth to several long lasting institutions that are completely unrelated to coffee. The origins of Lloyd's of London, one of the largest insurance companies in the world today, may be traced to the Edward Lloyd's Café where insurers used to get the lists of ships at sea and offer to insure them. Poetry came from Will's coffeehouse, foreign news from St. James coffeehouse, and arts from White's. Richard Steele sought to capitalize on the opportunities afforded by the special interest coffeehouses by planting correspondents at various cafés. He collected local stories and anthologized a collection of stories from various coffeehouses. In 1709, he founded the literary and society journal *The Tatler*, which lives on today after several reincarnations.

Stephen Morrissey judging at the 2011 WBC.

Fast forward a few centuries. London's comeback in the coffee world is being spearheaded by a world class coffee couple and their close friends, and aided by a few energetic Antipodeans.

Anette Moldvaer and James Hoffmann met in 2005 while Anette was working for Mercanta, an importer of specialty coffee in London, and had the opportunity to train James in the art of roasting and tasting coffee. During an eventful 2007, Anette took her first competing stab at the World Cup Tasters Championship and won the world title. A few months later, James won the U.K. Barista Championship for the second consecutive year and went on to win the World Barista Championship (WBC) in Tokyo.

With such a collection of accolades, Anette and James set their sights on a new goal: to finally launch their own coffee roasting company. They got together with an Irish lad, Stephen Morrissey, and started Square Mile Coffee Roasters in east London (for those not familiar with London terminology, the Square Mile refers to the core of the city of London and its business district). Stephen did not disappoint either. He won the 2008 WBC in Copenhagen, and later went to manage the training program for Intelligentsia Coffee in Chicago. Faced with the prospect of losing world domination and winning streak, Anette and James convinced their friend Gwilym Davies, owner of Prufrock Coffee, to compete in 2009. Gwilym, who was inspired to enter the coffee business after experiencing New Zealand's coffee culture, was initially skeptical. However, he took the plunge in the hopes that competing would give him an opportunity to improve his technique. Lo and behold, Gwilym won the 2009 WBC in Atlanta with a presentation in which he let the judges

Gwilym Davies competing at the 2009 WBC.

DIS-LOYALTY CARD

Complete this tour of East London's emerging coffee scene to claim a free coffee from the World Barista Champion Gwilym Davies @ Prufrock.

THE ESPRESSO ROOM

CLIMPSON & SONS

taylor st baristas

dose

nüde espresso

PITCH 42 @ WHITECROSS MKT

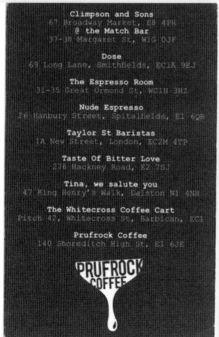

Climpson and Sons
67 Broadway Market, E8 4PH
@ the Match Bar
37-38 Margaret St, W1G 0JF

Dose
69 Long Lane, Smithfields, EC1A 9EJ

The Espresso Room
31-35 Great Ormond St, WC1N 3HZ

Nude Espresso
26 Hanbury Street, Spitalfields, E1 6QR

Taylor St Baristas
1A New Street, London, EC2M 4TP

Taste Of Bitter Love
276 Hackney Road, E2 7SJ

Tina, we salute you
47 King Henry's Walk, Dalston N1 4NH

The Whitecross Coffee Cart
Pitch 42, Whitecross St, Barbican, EC1

Prufrock Coffee
140 Shoreditch High St, E1 6JE

PRUFROCK COFFEE

effectively design the signature beverage by choosing the kind of texture, mouth feel and sweetness of the drink. To further promote the coffee culture in east London, Gwilym invented the now renowned "disloyalty card": if you visit eight *different* cafés in the neighborhood, Gwilym will make you a free cup of coffee.

James blogs and tweets often on all topics coffee, from preparation techniques, the importance of crema, the definition of macchiato, the various aspects of barista competitions, to the need for more coffee-related science. His blog (www.jimseven.com) has won several awards in the coffee world and is followed closely by coffee professionals worldwide. At Square Mile, Anette continues to be in charge of the roasting.

With a growing number of specialty roasters in and around London that also include Monmouth Coffee and the Stafford-based HasBean Coffee, hip new cafés are popping up everywhere. This is where the Antipodeans come into the picture.

Literally speaking, an Antipodean is someone who comes from exactly the other side of the earth. In London, the definition is relaxed a little bit to refer affectionately to Aussies and Kiwis who have come to set up businesses in London. With the help of certain labor laws that facilitate stints in London, the Antipodeans have taken to establish in London the same readily available high quality coffee culture that they enjoy back home in Australia and New Zealand. Because rents in London are ridiculously exorbitant, cafés are typically small. However, they are cozy and bustling places that attract people to socialize over good coffee and food all day long. One of these cafés, Kaffeine, recently won the designation Best European Café.

James predicts, perhaps wishfully, that in response to this wave of Antipodean-influenced cafés there will soon be more English-run cafés with more of an English atmosphere. Apparently, this would entail a little more emphasis on brewed coffee rather than espresso. In the summer of 2010, James and Anette took this idea to an extreme by briefly opening an experimental café, Penny University, that did not serve espresso-based drinks. The experiment garnered much attention. Now we are anxiously waiting for their next move in the coffee retail business.

There is no doubt that London sports a rather happening coffee scene today if you know where to go. On a personal level, London was one of the gratifying surprises of my coffee journey. ✍

James Hoffman and Anette Moldvaer on a coffee farm in Agrado, Colombia

SCANDANAVIA: The World's Most Caffeinated Countries

WHEN COFFEE FIRST ARRIVED IN SWEDEN, King Gustav III (1746-92) decided to prove "scientifically" that it has deleterious effects on health. His "clinical trial" involved identical twins who were convicted murderers serving life in prison: one was instructed to drink three pots of coffee every day, while the other only tea in the same quantity. To boost the credibility of his methodology, Gustav summoned two physicians to oversee the experiment. Unfortunately for Gustav, before he could publish his "scientific" findings, he was mur-

dered at the opera and the two trusted doctors passed away long before the prisoners. The tea drinker succumbed at the age of 83 and the coffee drinker a few years later, thus leaving Gustav's theory inconclusive at best. This was the most entertaining anecdote in the otherwise tempestuous early years of coffee in Sweden, which implicated draconian measures to prohibit coffee followed by heavy taxes on the brew. Those attempts seemed to have only intensified the coffee obsessions of the Swedes and other Scandinavians.

Coffee Collective in Copenhagen

Today, led by the Finns and the Norwegians, the Scandinavians are the highest per capita consumers of coffee on the planet (though some note that since the vast majority of coffee in Scandinavia is prepared in pots as opposed to espresso machines, it is unclear how much of the coffee is consumed by people versus kitchen sinks). While the high consumption may not be all that surprising given the long and severe Scandinavian winters, more unexpected is that six of the first seven world barista champions are from this part of the world—four from Denmark and two from Norway. This discovery piqued my interest and provided an excuse to visit one of my favorite regions in the world.

After many discussions with coffee professionals from all over Scandinavia, the following emerges as the best summary of the differences among Scandinavian coffee cultures. Norway, a beer drinking country until 100 years ago, has better water and a clientele with higher awareness and willingness to pay for better coffee. In fact, the Norwegians purchase a disproportionate amount of the award-winning Cup of Excellence coffees. Denmark, on the other hand, has better milk. While a crazy core of coffee nerds in Copenhagen is pushing the limits on coffee preparation and winning world championships, they will readily admit that the general Danish

Mellqvist Café: a favorite spot for locals in Stockholm.

Tim Wendelboe in front of his café in Oslo, Norway.

public does not enjoy a particularly pronounced coffee culture. The Swedes are faster at catching on to stylish trends, resulting in the large number of Italian-style bars that prevail throughout the country, especially Stockholm. While the Finns may drink more coffee than the others, the consensus seems to be that coffee *"just tastes different there."*

A visit with Tim Wendelboe at the café and roastery in Oslo that bears his name offers an insightful glimpse into Scandinavian coffee culture. Wendelboe is the 2004 World Barista Champion. He describes his overwhelming feeling upon winning the world title as one of *"relief,"* having placed second in two previous years. His recent book, *Coffee with Tim Wendelboe,* is an excellent compendium of both his vast repository of coffee-related knowledge and some of his strong opinions. He is known worldwide for his excellent roasts and in particular, for pushing the limits on lighter roasts. His café is located on a relatively quiet street of Oslo which makes it more a showcase for his roasts than a bustling café. According to Wendelboe, Norwegians have off-the-charts standards when it comes to coffee quality, and even the beans sold in supermarkets are of relatively high quality.

In addition to Wendelboe's beans, coffee lovers in Oslo are spoiled by other first-rate roasters, such as the much larger roaster Solberg and Hansen and cafés founded by Robert Thoresen, the first World Barista Champion, such as Mocca and Java. Wendelboe explains that when coffee first arrived in Norway in the late 17th century, the beverage choices in the country were rather slim. Because water was not safe to drink and the laws permitted anyone to brew their own alcoholic drinks, it was a pretty inebriated society. The local churches played a big role in promoting the role of coffee and established a tradition of "church coffee" which to this day involves gatherings on Sunday afternoons around coffee.

In the 1990's espresso became more popular in Norway and the local coffee professionals started working on improving their espresso-brewing technique. That led to the invention of a competition format consisting of a 15-minute presentation where the barista makes four espressos, four cappuccinos and four signature drinks. In 2000 this became the format of the first WBC that was held in Monte Carlo, with twelve countries participating.

After ceding the first world title to the Norwegians, a few coffee fanatics in Copenhagen consorted to master the art of competing. Between 2001 and 2006, they managed to create a coffee legacy by winning four world titles. These competitors came from Café Europa 1989 (on the main pedestrian thoroughfare of Copenhagen) and Estate Coffee, closer to the main train station. Out of the latter café emerged a team led by the 2006 World Barista Champion Klaus Thomsen that founded the Coffee Collective, the leader in exploring single origins and light roasts in Denmark.

Located in a residential neighborhood of Copenhagen, the stated goal of the Coffee Collective is to *"provide people with an exceptional coffee experience."* The "Collective" refers to the idea of bringing together the three main components in the coffee chain: growers, roasters and baristas. Customers who enter the small café are always assured of the most thoughtful advice about their coffee needs.

The Collective conducts cuppings of their roasts on a regular basis to further educate its clientele about sensory subtleties that render coffee such a complex commodity.

Sweden's café scene is a constantly evolving potpourri. Stockholm abounds with charming cafés, some of which serve the traditional brewed coffee that is still preferred by many Swedes (though it should not be compared to its U.S. counterpart because the Swedish brew tends to be much more flavorful). Many cafés are inspired by the Italian café style. For example, baristas at Sosta Coffee act and speak Italian. Mellqvist Café and Bar, which was unanimously recommended by all the locals I spoke with, adds a Swedish twist to the Italian espresso bar by efficiently serving a very traditional breakfast to folks on the move. When Johan and Nystrom opened a roastery a few years ago, they made a splash because they were the first roaster to open in the Stockholm area in a few decades. A recent addition to the café scene is Drop Coffee in the hip Södermalm district where customers may well receive an animated explanation about the differences between specialty coffee and traditional Italian roasts.

Many of the vanguards of Sweden's specialty coffee industry are outside Stockholm. Beginning far up north in the skiing town of Åre, Eva and Per Nordell quit their teaching jobs several years ago to start the Åre Kafferosteri roastery in their home. In Helsingborg, a city that is as close to Copenhagen as it is to any major Swedish city, Anne Lunell runs the Koppi microroastery and coffee shop. Her fiancée and Koppi co-owner Charles

Nystrand's win as the Swedish National Barista Champion in 2005 inspired her to try her luck the following year. After winning the Swedish national title in 2006, Anne went on to place fourth at the WBC in Bern the same year, marking Sweden's top achievement on the world scene. Along with roasters such as Da Matteo in Gotheborg and Brasset in Malmö, these roasters and baristas are trying to introduce the latest trends in the coffee world as alternative Swedish coffee experiences to the traditional Italian espresso.

The Swedish milk industry is credited with helping to energize the country's barista profession in an unexpected way. In 2000, Swedish milk companies joined forces to form a consortium that copyrighted the term "Latte Art" in Sweden and offered a series of barista training courses that focused more on the milkier drinks than on espresso. To lure prospective baristas, the first course in the series was free. After the training program ended in 2008, Arla, the largest milk company in Sweden developed a new and slightly more expensive milk product that is particularly suited for making lattes. Lest you think it was merely a marketing ploy of putting a nice photo of latte art on the carton, I was assured that the milk is actually the result of careful research that found the right balance between the amount of protein and milk fat to ensure longer-lasting foam. If nothing else, seeing an exquisite latte art photo every time you open the fridge is surely worth a few more kronors.

No portrayal of Scandinavian coffee culture is complete without mentioning the Swedish *fika*, loosely translated as "coffee break." Around 3pm on weekdays, office workers all over Sweden will gather for the fika. One person will take charge of preparing the coffee and another will ensure there is appropriate pastry, preferably one of the heavenly Swedish cinnamon rolls (a much more delectable version of the kind that Ikea exports worldwide through its cafeterias), or sometimes a smörgås. On weekends, excitedly impatient children urge their parents to perform the fika ritual at home or with their local community. The Swedes are open minded. You may have tea at fika if you must, there is flexibility on the type of sweet baked item or savory sandwich served. You may even do fika at 2pm if that suits your needs better. As long as you are getting together with your friends to socialize, you have captured the essence of this defining Swedish tradition. ✎

Roasting at Drop Coffee in Stockholm

Enjoying coffee in Stockholm

ICELAND: The World's Most Close-Knit Coffee Community

ON A FRIGID WINTER MORNING IN 1985, VICTOR ALLEN, one of the pioneers of specialty coffee in America, was holding a coffee roasting course in Madison, Wisconsin. The only person who succeeded in braving the cold that day was Addý Hedinsdottir, an Icelandic woman who was living in Madison while her husband was obtaining his doctorate at the university. On that momentous day, Addý not only received a private roasting lesson from Allen and became hooked on coffee, but also found a mentor in Allen. When she returned to Iceland a few years later, she brought one of Allen's old roasters with her, setting the stage for an extremely energetic specialty coffee community in her home country.

In 1990, Addý founded her coffee company, *Kaffitár*, initially roasting coffee and selling to cafés and supermarkets. The name Kaffitár, which means "a tear of coffee" in Icelandic, is inspired by the tradition of always having coffee ready for visitors, a hallmark of Icelandic hospitality. She decided to open her own cafés in 1995. Today, Kaffitár cafés greet you with an excellent cup of coffee anywhere from Reykjavík's airport to its downtown and national museum. With bright hues, playful decorations, and eye-catching coffee paraphernalia, the cafés are striking.

One of Addý's first hires was Sonja Grant who came with a befitting resume that included careers as a carpenter and children's equestrian coach. Both Addý and Sonja have since become fixtures in the international coffee community. Addý is often on the road visiting the farms that supply her coffee and participating in coffee tastings around the world. Sonja trains baristas in Iceland and around the world. She is also one of the main forces that shaped the World Barista Championship (WBC). In 2012, she will serve as

Sonja Grant and her pink roaster

One of the many colorful Kaffitár cafés

the chairwoman of the World Coffee Events, the organization that runs all the coffee competitions.

Iceland has been no slacker on the world barista scene. In the first WBC, Iceland's Erla Kristinsdóttir took the second spot, a feat that was repeated by Åsa Petterson in 2003.

Coffee culture runs very deeply in Iceland. Until the 1987 legalization of beer, coffee had been the drink of choice at every social gathering. When real coffee was not readily available and Icelanders had to settle for substitutes such as chicory, serving the real thing was a sign of going the extra mile on hospitality. The coffee was typically brewed rather strong and bitter. There are amusing stories about the Icelandic's bizarre preferences when it comes to coffee, such as a café in Reykjavík that specialized in serving expired beans from Sweden. Coffee has also played an important part in politics. As politicians campaigned in the countryside, they had to accept a cup of coffee on every farm they visited lest they be considered rude. In the town of Selfoss, Bjarni Harðarson even opened a coffee and bookshop after he was forced to resign from the Icelandic parliament (after he had unintentionally cc'ed his entire political party on an email espousing a few harsh opinions about its leaders). Priests and doctors were also routinely served coffee during home visits, which led to their own health problems. These customs are the root of the expression "*tíu dropar*" (ten drops), which means just enough coffee to warm you up before you go on your way, but not to over-caffeinate you.

In 2008, Sonja and her Kaffitár colleague and two-time Icelandic national barista champion Ingibjörg Jóna Sigurðardóttir (better known as Imma) started a new café and micro-roaster called Kaffismiðja Íslands, or "coffee workshop of the island." The founding vision of Kaffismiðja was to combine a café, roastery and coffee workshop into a one-stop training center for young baristas. Kaffismiðja is located in an unassuming building in a quiet neighborhood in downtown Reykjavík, without even a sign on the entrance.

While Kaffismiðja revels in simplicity with its few tables, old-fashioned record player and homemade pastries, it boasts an eye-popping accoutrement: a neon pink roasting machine that is an oddity in a sea of macho-colored roasting machines. In Iceland's female dominated coffee industry, Sonja and Imma wanted to make a statement by special ordering a roaster from Giesen Roasters that matched one of Sonja's flamboyant dresses. Their expression of coffee is also unique. In the last couple of years, Kaffismiðja's focus on celebrating coffees from two micro-lots in the Huila district of Colombia has created a very direct relationship between its clientele and the farms.

Ingibjörg Jóna Sigurðardóttir (Imma) preparing coffee at Kaffismiðja Íslands

A coffee-cup clock at Kaffitar

Kaffismiðja's concept and execution are clearly working. The cozy café is typically full and has been recognized as the best café in Reykjavík for three years in a row!

There is no better way to experience the close-knit coffee community of Iceland than walking down the streets of Reykjavík with Sonja and from time to time being stopped by her customers or others who recognize her. During her guided tour of the city and its cafés, we visited Kaffi Mokka, Reykjavík's oldest café that dates back to 1958, as well as her original Kaffitár stomping grounds where the baristas, many of whom had been her students, greeted her warmly. Sonja explained that in the early days of specialty coffee in Iceland, the Icelandic language did not even have a word for barista. Because adopting foreign words is not customary in Icelandic, she and her partner invented, in preparation for the first national barista championship, the word *kaffibarþjónn* (literally, "coffee bartender"), which is now the commonly accepted word for barista.

Sonja also plays a significant role in the story of the Ferrer family of coffee champions. When one of the longtime Kaffitár customers, Yrsa Þórðardóttir, mentioned to Sonja a few years ago that her son Tumi Ferrer would like a job at Kaffitár, she was pleased and soon began to train him in all aspects of the art. Not long after Tumi became enamored with coffee and its artisanship, his younger sister Ingibjörg followed suit. In 2010, Ingibjörg won the Icelandic Barista Championship at the age of 19 and became the youngest competitor at the WBC in London. Simultaneously, Tumi won the national cupping competition that earned him a trip to London as well.

Upon seeing his children's successes, Yrsa's husband Carlos Ferrer, an ever so curious and adventuresome soul, decided that it was high time that he flirted with a coffee competition. The only suitable competition left in 2010 was the Coffee in Good Spirits Competition where he had to create an Irish coffee and a signature drink. Carlos, a minister who had dabbled in teaching elementary school and Web 2.0 at the University of Iceland, trained for six weeks by tapping into the expertise of the pros in his family and borrowing from their training resources. To the shock and amusement of the Icelandic barista community, the relative coffee rookie ended up winning the national championship! Needless to say, Tumi and Ingibjörg were accompanied to London by a parental chaperone. Thankfully, Carlos behaved well in London and even made his children proud by placing eighth. In 2011, Tumi kept up the family's reputation by winning the Icelandic Barista Championship. Despite their lofty titles, the Ferrers insist that the culinary authority in the household is Yrsa who had studied hotel management in Strasbourg France. She is also a coffee enthusiast. As Tumi

Carlos preparing his
signature drink;
above, Tumi, Ingibjorg
and Carlos Ferrer.

puts it: *"Her love for robust and dark coffees is perfectly understandable considering that she spent two decades of her life in France."* When the Ferrers hosted a barista party, Yrsa happily whipped up espressos for everyone using a push-button Nespresso machine.

I was fortunate to sample Carlos' explosive signature drink from the 2010 competition at the Ferrers' summerhouse outside the city of Selfoss, a completely secluded and picturesque house with stunning views from all the windows. The signature drink was based on a volcanic syrup that includes moscovato sugar, some paprika and chilly peppers. After the syrup was shaken vigorously with coffee, it was poured into a glass and topped off with a local Lava Beer and a plum tomato dipped in volcanic syrup hanging off a cocktail stick.

Carlos' feisty concoction was the perfect prelude to the ebullient dinner conversation that followed. Not surprisingly, coffee was the central theme. Topics flowed from the different brewing techniques they are able to employ at their home to how Ingibjörg's signature drink was inspired by her dad's Christmas menu that included mango sorbet and chocolate delicacies. The discussion reached its crescendo when Carlos served his sublime Irish coffees to everyone—how to choose a coffee that will yield a perfectly balanced Irish coffee was hotly debated. The lively scene from that evening was the most vivid portrayal of Icelandic coffee culture complemented by the best Icelandic hospitality anyone could imagine. ✎

ISRAEL: A Crossroad of Coffee Cultures

IF YOU ARE LOOKING FOR ANCIENT HISTORY, THERE IS NO BETTER PLACE to visit than Israel. While the country doesn't conjure up images of gourmet coffee, it turns out that thanks to many waves of immigration, Israel offers a unique opportunity to tour a living history of coffee that can all be done in just a few hours.

Begin with a taste of the birthplace of coffee at any authentic Ethiopian grocery shop found in any of Israel's many Ethiopian neighborhoods. Ethiopian Jews have been immigrating to Israel for decades. Political instability in Ethiopia led to the most recent emigration wave of the 1990's. Alongside many spices, these neighborhood grocery stores dependably feature several sacks of green coffee beans. As the shop owner explains, his clientele follows the Ethiopian custom of roasting the beans at home on a frying pan as part of the traditional coffee ceremony. If you linger long enough in the store, you will likely end up being invited to someone's home to experience a time-honored full coffee ceremony.

The next obligatory stop on the historical tour mirrors the path of coffee discovery and brings you to a Yemenite neighborhood. Jews from Yemen began immigrating to Israel almost four decades before Israel became an independent state in 1948. The most recent immigration, "Operation Magic Carpet" of 1949, is an extraordinary story. With the tacit agreement of the government of Yemen, Israel successfully deployed 380 flights to airlift 450,000 Jews from Aden, Yemen. The operation was kept completely secret until its completion, an unimaginable feat in today's digitally connected world. Yemenite immigrants have established one of the richest subcultures of contemporary Israeli society. Their special preparation of coffee is particularly noteworthy. According to Pnina Shar'abi (whose father used to trade coffee in Yemen before he immigrated to Israel), because all the coffee beans in Yemen were saved for export, the resourceful locals developed a drink from the powderized coffee cherry pulp called *kisher* (or *gisher*, depending on your pronunciation skills). The

Yemenites add to this rather weak coffee drink a spice mix called *hawayij* that includes cinnamon, ginger and cardamom. The intoxicating aroma of the resulting beverage easily captures anyone's heart.

From Yemen coffee infiltrated the Arab peninsula, then controlled by the Ottoman Empire. The Arab coffee drinking experience may be observed in any of the Arab-populated areas in Israel. A mere forty-five minute drive from Tel Aviv will take you to Jerusalem where you will see many Arabs sipping their coffee and smoking their pipes as you stroll through the Old City. If you are in the Tel Aviv area, amble down the beach promenade of Tel Aviv to the adjoining city of Yaffo. There you will find a number of cafés that serve authentic Turkish coffee that is true to the slogan *"black as hell, strong as death and sweet as love."* These cafés also provide an amiably relaxing environment where Jews and Arabs bond over coffee.

The Turks spread coffee to the rest of Europe where several European coffee cultures evolved and flourished. Because many Israelis emigrated from Turkey, Greece, Bulgaria and Northern Africa, they regularly prepare Turkish coffee at home, often multiple times a day.

Being a magnet to immigrants from all parts

Pnina Shar'abi demonstrates the full gamut of Yemenite coffee beverages.

Arabs in Yaffo discuss matters of the day with coffee and hookahs.

Café Tamar

of Europe, Israel has it all, from high-end Italian espresso to Viennese-style coffee drinks. In the early days, the Israeli intelligentsia used to congregate at Café Casit on Dizengof Street, in similar fashion as their counterparts in Vienna or Paris.

Today, Tel Aviv brims with happening cafés that beckon passersby to stop in and linger. A good place to start touring is the trendy Sheinkin Street in southern Tel Aviv and its adjacent Neve Tzedek neighborhood. On Sheinkin, you have the opportunity to step back in time at Café Tamar. This café has been around since 1941 and has managed to preserve its character. Even though the furnishings are simple and dated and the decor is a potpourri of posters and illustrations collected over the years, this remains the preferred meeting venue for authors, judges, actors and professors. The real story here is the proprietor, Sara Stern, who darts around the tables giving each patron an honest piece of her mind. Sara met her late husband while serving in the British army "in the sands of Egypt," and has maintained her scruffy edge ever since. The mayor of Tel Aviv recently organized a party in City Hall in celebration of Sara's 85th birthday. While every imaginable superlative was bestowed upon Sara, mayor Ron Huldai's description was the most telling: "*Each time I come, Sara gets on my nerves. 'What's new?' 'Is everything okay?' And then come the complaints about the property tax, the inspectors, the street sweepers and the tow trucks, and then she plops down some poppy cake even though I actually prefer cheesecake.*"

Besides showcasing coffee customs from around the world, Israel has its own coffee specialties. You can typically ask for a "*cafe hafuch*" (literally, "upside down coffee") and receive a drink that approximates a cappuccino. The origin of the term '*café hafuch*' is unclear, but you can think of it as a timeless concept where some sort of coffee is poured into a cup of hot or frothed milk. Before espresso became popular in Israel, the coffee would have been a shot of instant coffee. Even today, if you are very unlucky or veer far off the beaten path, you may still encounter this "classic" version. Israelis have also invented a coffee drink called '*café barad*' (literally, "hailstone coffee"), to combat their sultry summers. It may best be described as a sweet and slushy cold coffee drink for grown-ups.

With over 30 outlets, Israel's leading local café chain Arcaffe exemplifies the fusion of different culinary traditions. Its mission explicitly identifies the goal of marrying the best of Italian coffee with the finest of French baked goods. After searching for macchiatones worldwide, I was flabbergasted to find one in an Arcaffe right in my childhood town! A macchiatone accompanied by a warm almond croissant at Arcaffe is a wonderful way to kick off any day on a high note, whether upon arrival at Israel's Ben Gurion airport or before boarding a departure flight.

Founder Sara Shemer recounted the process she followed to select an Italian partner for her venture. After receiving one hundred responses to her business plan from Italian coffee companies, she had to enlist the help of a father of one of her friends who is a coffee trader in Trieste. The gentleman, who happened to be visiting Israel for Passover, helped her narrow down the field to five finalists from which the winner from Livorno was selected. Once the coffee supplier was settled, finding the French partner became a relative piece of cake.

In addition to Arcaffe, there are several other local coffee chains in Israel such as Aroma Coffee, Caffe Joe's, and Café Café, each sporting its own Italian-style signature drink or twist on customer service. As in any respectable establishment in Israel, there is always an assortment of nice light meals and baked items available to accompany your coffee. Cafés in Israel are busy at all hours of the day. It is very typical to see cafés bustling even past midnight. And they do not all serve decaf at those hours.

Israeli coffee culture also has bizarre idiosyncrasies that defy explanation. One prime example is the Israeli infatuation with *Nescafé* instant coffee from Elite, the local coffee and chocolate maker. The roots of the infatuation may be traced back to most Israelis' initial strong coffee exposure during their military service. In the army, coffee breaks are the only times when you finally have a chance to bond

Merchants in the Old City of Jerusalem have their coffee delivered by special couriers.

with your fellow soldiers and to rest without anyone ordering you around. The coffee choices boil down to either the army-supplied black coffee or the far more alluring instant coffee. However, producing a cup of instant coffee often involved overcoming seemingly insurmountable obstacles. The first step involves locating someone with a stash of instant coffee. Then one must mobilize resources to rise to the challenges of finding a container of milk that has not gone bad in the hot weather and tracking down a clean cup and boiled water. All in all the task could easily take up to an hour, depending on what connections you have with the higher-ups (or their assistants) at the army base. The cleansing benefits of Elite instant coffee on one's digestive system have been well-documented. Hence, seeing Israeli travelers carry a can of this stuff on their overseas trips should raise no eyebrows. Incidentally, *Nescafé* is typically abbreviated as 'nes', which means miracle in Hebrew. Another strong reason to go all out for this stuff.

The Café Professor

If you have ever wondered about the theory of bargaining, you should talk to Ariel Rubinstein, a world-renowned professor of economics who laid the foundation for the field. And if you want to meet him, you will most likely find him at a café. Ariel, who spends most of his time in Tel Aviv but is a frequent visitor to New York City, holds most of his meetings with students and colleagues in cafés around the world. Not just any café though. They need to have a special atmosphere and the right lighting and acoustics, and feel as cozy and unpretentious as one's family room where one can sink into a state of deep thought.

Ariel is so passionate about his cafés and has traveled so extensively that he has compiled a beautiful poster entitled *"Coffee Places Where You Can Think."* The poster samples cafés from around the world that satisfy his criteria of appeal. You can find the poster as well as many other coffee-related recommendations on his web site (arielrubinstein. tau.ac.il). He is pleased to see his poster adorn the walls of many of the featured cafés.

Rubinstein's café poster hanging in Tola'at Sefarim, Tel Aviv.

The shocker is that Ariel does not actually like coffee! In his words, *"The aroma causes me a headache, and the bitter taste makes my facial muscles contract."* His antidote is a *"one-quarter coffee"*: one quarter of a cup filled with drip coffee and three quarters water and some milk. If it were possible, he would have a quarter of a teaspoon of instant coffee wherever he goes but alas, some cafés will simply not stoop that low. Amusingly, his unique personal dilemma poses an interesting problem in economics: what should be the price of such a diluted cup of coffee?

After visiting many cafés in the United States, Ariel has made some (non-scientific!) observations about American culture. Initially, he thought he should not receive a discount for his coffee because the cost for the seller is not really much lower than the cost of a regular cup of coffee. In fact, it often takes him more time to explain to the barista what he wants. He is also willing to pay more just to get the right drink. He has published his rather surprising "research results" in the Israeli press. Whenever the cost of a cup of coffee was less than $2, there was a much higher chance that the barista would offer him a discount. But when the price was higher, he was rarely offered a discount. When the price of a cup of coffee was more than $4 he never received a discount. Ariel summarized his conclusions: *"Despite their low pay and fear of losing the source of their income, there are many people in America who are sensitive to justice as well as profits. These people may not have worked in financial firms on Wall Street, but they are no less part of America than CEOs with golden parachutes. In short, even America isn't exactly as I imagined it to be. That too, is a source of hope."*

Café Puah, in the heart of the Flea Market in Jaffa.

Atop Mount Carmel in the northern city of Haifa, Cafe Capiot overlooks the Haifa Harbor.

The University of Cafés

Tel Aviv, Israel's first and largest city, celebrated its centennial in 2009. In its honor, Ariel Rubinestein published an article in the leading Israeli newspaper, *Yediot Achronot,* celebrating Tel Aviv's cafés and elegantly articulating his philosophy of cafés. The English translation below is by Ayelet Dekel.

Tel Aviv at 100 years old is bustling with culture. A large research university is situated north of the Yarkon River. Although I am a member of the faculty of that university, I feel like I belong to another wonderful institution established by the first Hebrew city: "The University of Tel Aviv Cafés." It is the only place where I can sit for long hours, sink into contemplation without interruption, write, delete and think.

Not every Tel Aviv café is included in our university. The criteria for acceptance are complex. First of all, it is a matter of light and shade; not too dark, not too bright. You need to feel that the place cuddles you in a homey pleasantness. Ideally, there is a tree to shade the windows on a sweltering day. It is important for there to be a small window to allow a refreshing breeze, rather than large openings for gusts of wind. The acoustics are also important: The conversations should converge among the interlocutors. The music must not be too loud, and of course the annoying newscasts should not resound every hour.

A sophisticated Italian espresso machine is not necessary in order to be part of our campus, and there is no need for the coffee beans to arrive via express mail from the coffee barons in Colombia. It is important that sitting in the coffeehouse does not require a binge of gluttony. It should be expected that the patrons of the place will remain even after slowly finishing the salad and drinking three mugs of coffee.

Some accuse our university of lacking research laboratories. Not exactly. We are located in the heart of the laboratory of life. Our researchers, primarily from the fields of social sciences and humanities, directly observe reality and are updated in real time. It would be an exaggeration to claim that we are connecting with the people, but we are certainly not sequestering ourselves in an ivory tower.

Our departments have names like Bugsy, Birnbaum, Beta, Sucar, Book Worm and Tamar, and are not named for mysterious donors. We engage in celebrating life and not in memorializing the dead. Our university does not pay salaries, but offers the ideal work setting for many. As for me, I have written more pages of satisfying work in the coffeehouses of Tel Aviv than in my opulent office.

In the The University of Cafés, no one demands that research must be useful. From the outset, there is an atmosphere of apparent idleness and lack of purpose at the coffeehouses, which is the suitable atmosphere for basic research. The system of promotions at our university is based on the breadth of the smiles of the café employees. There are no appointments committees. There are no rectors or deans. Every young person is gladly accepted, at least as readily as a tenured professor. There is a real interdisciplinary tradition at our university. Only here can you find a true encounter between a mathematician, economist and historian.

Our motto is: Freedom, Education and Openness. Academic freedom is a reality and not just an empty slogan unfathomed by many of those who recite it. We have absolute independence in our establishment. With us, there is no attempt to separate academia and politics, and there is no demand for political correctness. Instead of keeping the door of the office open when someone of the opposite sex enters the room, it is considered inappropriate behavior in our coffeehouses to ignore flirtation from the opposite sex.

It is said that the universities in Israel are deteriorating. This crisis is bypassing the University of Tel Aviv Cafés, which continues to prosper according to any international criterion. Perhaps our sister cafés in Berlin and Vienna measure up to us. London and New York definitely fall short in comparison. In brief, we are placed well within the top ten, a status that no Israeli university dreams of attaining.

Sometimes, as evening approaches, I pass by a Tel Aviv Café, see the regulars, with or without a laptop, alone or in a group, and look enviously at them. But then I remember that I am one of them. What a good feeling. 🖎

THE UNITED STATES OF AMERICA

Coffee history of the United States does not feature scintillating tales of the bean's arrival via dangerous liaisons, extravagant parties, or reckless abandonment after failed sieges. Coffee has been around since the founding of the country. In fact, the Boston Tea Party that involved throwing sacks of tea into the Boston Harbor in protest of the king's taxation policies only fueled the patriotic sentiments of early American settlers and strengthened their national identity with coffee.

The United States is the largest consumer of coffee in the world (and will remain so until more Chinese kick their tea habit). It is also geographically close to the main coffee growing regions of the world. As a result, the story of coffee in the United States during the two centuries immediately following the Boston Tea Party had more to do with the economics of coffee and involvement in the civil strife of the coffee producing countries than with concern for coffee quality. American corporations mastered the sciences of mass production and advertising, and of squeezing every penny of profit out of its hopelessly caffeinated consumers. By the 1950's, American coffee had justifiably earned the ignominious reputation of tasting like dishwater.

It took a Dutch immigrant and the 1960's counter-culture atmosphere of Berkeley, California to start turning the tide around. Alfred Peet opened a store that generated excitement about quality coffee and inspired a new generation of coffee fanatics and professionals. Peet demonstrated that coffee need not come in tin cans and should not be evaluated by the eloquence of advertising taglines. Among Peet's many followers were the founders of a coffee up-start in Seattle called Starbucks. By the mid 1990's, Starbucks stores were popping up at dizzying rates on every street corner, sometimes even across the street from each other. Before long, from established coffee markets in Europe to virgin territories in Asia, the Starbucks mermaid logo had become as recognizable internationally as McDonald's iconic golden arch.

Peets and Starbucks were only the first step in unleashing a wave of American coffeepreneurs who began scouting the world for the best beans and fostering dynamic café, barista, and roaster cultures that are envied worldwide. As a result of their initiatives, passion, and perseverance, exceptional coffee (by world standards) may be found in the United States today if you know where to go.

The next chapters offer an abbreviated chronicle of the vicissitude of American coffee culture through three "coffee waves." In particular, we highlight the key contributions of some of the pioneers and their protégés who have been instrumental in blazing adventurous trails and spurring inevitable waves of change and innovation.

Samuel Purvis (foreground)
and Devin Chapman tend bar
at Coava Coffee Roasters in
Portland, Oregon.

A NATION BORN INTO COFFEE

COFFEE DRINKING IN THE UNITED STATES BECAME A MATTER OF NATIONAL PRIDE long before Starbucks started to pop up on every street corner around the world. On December 16, 1773, two hundred men, some disguised as Indians, stormed three ships of the British East India Company and tossed all 300-hundred plus chests of stored tea into the Boston Harbor. In what became known as the Boston Tea Party, this watershed event was a protest against taxation without representation and helped fuel the American Revolution.

From that moment on, renouncing tea and embracing coffee took on patriotic significance. Revolutionaries such as George Washington, Paul Revere and John Adams chose coffeehouses as preferred venues to convene. Even the first public reading of the *Declaration of Independence* was held outside the Merchant's Coffee House in Philadelphia. John Adams, who later became the second president of the United States, brought it to a personal level when he stated in a letter to his wife Abigail: "*Tea must be universally renounced. I myself must be weaned, and the sooner the better.*" A few years later, when Abigail explained to John that she and a few other angry Boston women had stormed a local warehouse that was holding back coffee and sugar supplies, she found sympathetic ears.

Things went downhill for a long time from those venerable roots. For almost two centuries, the history of coffee in the United States had less to do with coffee quality than mass production, fluctuating market prices, and creative advertising. Ultimately, American coffee companies relied on sexual overtones in radio and TV ads to sell a product that was so hideous that it forced an entire generation of baby boomers to flee to Coca Cola for their caffeine fixes.

A model of the Jabez Burns roaster, on display at Sweet Maria's in Oakland, California.

While the Europeans were inventing more sophisticated coffee preparation methods during the first half of the 19th century, Americans were stuck with a drink that needed considerable milk and sugar to be palatable. In those earlier days, Americans bought green coffee beans, roasted them at home on a frying pan, and then ground them with a mortar and pestle. The ground beans were boiled in water to yield a drink. Ingenuity was required to clear the drink from floating sediments. Recommendations from the experts included using egg yolk or cod, not exactly aromas you associated with a great cup of coffee, to remove the grounds. Incredulously, the average American consumed six times more coffee than their European counterparts back then.

The movement towards standardization and mass marketing of coffee began around the end of the Civil War in the middle of the 19th century. In his book *Uncommon Grounds*, Mark Pendergrast skillfully describes the blow-by-blow downward spiral as the American coffee industry sank into an abysmal state of affairs.

The invention of an easy to operate coffee roaster by an immigrant from England named Jabez Burns was the initial catalyst. Over the next fifteen years and aided by the invention of the durable paper bag just a few years earlier, Burns was able to sell his roasters to small business owners around the country. The ability to purchase roasted beans drastically reduced coffee preparation time.

Then came the coffee dynasties that would rule the American coffee industry and shape the culture surrounding it. The first dynasty was founded in 1864 by John Arbuckle in Pittsburgh, Pennsylvania. Creating a branded coffee and selling coffee in paper bags on a large scale, Arbuckle essentially introduced standardization into the coffee business. Jim Folger from Nantucket Massachusetts, who initially ventured out West to dig for gold with his brothers, founded his coffee business in 1865 in San Francisco and ultimately fared better than his siblings. By the turn of the 20th century, Hills Brothers and MJB (a much catchier name than the original M. J. Brandenstein & Co.) began challenging Folger's domination of the West Coast. In 1878, Chase and Sanborn joined forces to start a coffee business in Boston that then expanded to Chicago and Montreal. Started in 1893 in Nashville Tennessee, Maxwell House was named after the Maxwell Hotel, the first venue willing to try out the new blend that was perfected by the company's founder Joel Cheek. The Maxwell fortunes shot up after President Theodore Roosevelt famously quipped *"good to the last drop"* when he was served the Maxwell blend during a visit to the Hermitage Resort in Nashville in 1907.

John Arbuckle from Pittsburgh was viewed as quite a trendsetter when he started selling his Ariosa brand coffee beans in brown paper bags. At first, mocked for such a ridiculous idea, his business became an immediate success and soon expanded nationwide. Arbuckle went even further and built a vertically integrated company that was quite ahead

The first espresso machine in the United States. Manufactured in 1902 and brought from Italy to Caffe Reggio in Greenwich Village in New York City, a café that has been open since 1927.

of its time. The company boasted its own green bean exporting businesses in Brazil and Mexico, its own shipping fleet, and even its own hospital for its employees at its Brooklyn New York plant. Arbuckle was also the first coffee seller to realize the impact of sophisticated advertising. His marketing campaigns emphasized the power of standardized coffee and featured ads ridiculing the failed attempts of housewives at roasting their own beans.

Ironically, the ultimate decline of Arbuckle came because the firm decided in 1921 not to pursue an aggressive nationwide marketing campaign. Arbuckle's coffee is still available for purchase today, though the online ads are targeted at a somewhat narrower audience: *"Everything the Cowboy came to trust; from the rich, full flavor to John Arbuckle's original premium item, the peppermint stick. Now you can once again enjoy the full-bodied, aromatic coffee that won the West."*

Beginning in 1885, the coffee industry in America got a serious kick in the rear from a fierce outside competitor. C.W. Post founded a company to sell his invention, Postum, a grain-based coffee substitute made from wheat bran and molasses. He then went on a marketing rampage that played off the fears of health conscious Americans who at the time had no idea of the real effects of coffee. His ads scared people by alluding to medical conditions such as "coffee heart," "coffee neuralgia," and "brain fag," and promised Postum as the panacea. Post regularly enjoyed a cup of coffee in private, though he would often spend a few days detoxifying himself with Postum. In a twist of events all too common for the business world, after Post's death his firm (which was renamed General Foods) purchased Maxwell House in 1928. General Foods then began profiting from the Maxwell line of coffees that Post had so viciously attacked. It took several more decades after that to wean Americans off Postum, which was finally discontinued in 2007.

Judging from the story of Gus Comstock, whatever the coffee giants were peddling to the public clearly could not have had much oomph. On January 11, 1927, Gus achieved a feat that earned him *"unequaled fame in the history of Otter Tail County, Minnesota."* Gus set out to reclaim his coffee drinking record that had recently been lost to a Texan who downed 72 cups of coffee in ten hours. He started at 7am and consumed the first 15 cups in the first hour. After five hours, he was checked by a doctor who declared him to be in good shape except for a mild fever. But later in the day he had to slow down and finally quit after consuming 75 cups. To put this in perspective, if Gus were to attempt this today at the local Starbucks with its typical drip coffee, he would be dead by lunchtime. Seventy-five cups of Starbucks' drip coffee contain 13.6 grams of pure caffeine, exceeding the five to ten grams that are considered a fatal oral dose.

Financial pressures in the next few decades forced the coffee giants to further reduce the quality of the coffee (by adding more

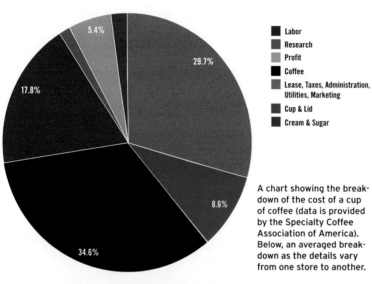

Labor
Research
Profit
Coffee
Lease, Taxes, Administration, Utilities, Marketing
Cup & Lid
Cream & Sugar

A chart showing the breakdown of the cost of a cup of coffee (data is provided by the Specialty Coffee Association of America). Below, an averaged breakdown as the details vary from one store to another.

COFFEE – 34.6%

CREAM & SUGAR – 2.2%

CUP & LID – 8.6%

LEASE, TAXES, ADMINISTRATION, UTILITIES, MARKETING – 29.7%

LABOR – 17.8%

PROFIT – 5.4%

Robusta beans to their blends, among other things) and make up for it with more entertaining advertising campaigns. The popularity of radio in the 1930's and of television two decades later helped stir the creative juices of many ads managers. In October 1932, Maxwell House introduced an hour-long radio show called *"The Maxwell House Show Boat"* that, needless to say, had nothing to do with a real boat. It featured comedy, music and drama. *"Welcome aboard, folks,"* the host would announce, *"Your ticket of admission is just your loyalty to Maxwell House Coffee."* By the beginning of 1933, the *Show Boat* had become the top-rated radio show. Concomitantly, Maxwell House announced a better blend and a five-cent cut in prices. The scheme worked and sales went up by 85% that year.

In 1935, Chase and Sanborn responded by launching the *"Major Bowes Amateur Hour,"* a radio show that traveled from city to city and featured local artists. The program delivered consistently high ratings until Mae West performed a couple of skits. In one of them, named "Adam and Eve in the Garden of Eden," she sultrily told her partner to *"get me a big one ... I feel like doin' a big apple!"* Within days, complaints from Catholic groups came pouring in. The Federal Communications Commission later deemed the broadcast *"vulgar and indecent"* and *"far below even the minimum standard which should control in the selection and production of broadcast programs."* Even though Mae was banned from radio for 12 years, Chase and Sanborn sales were not adversely affected. By the time the 1990's rolled around, Taster's Choice had buoyed to the top of the instant coffee market by the much more subtle sexual innuendo between Sharon and her neighbor Tony.

Fortunately, in the mid-1960's a Dutch immigrant came to the rescue and reminded Americans that coffee can have great flavor. He started reversing the downward trend of coffee quality in the country from his base in Berkeley, California. ✑

SAN FRANCISCO BAY AREA: Seeds of a Coffee Revolution

A FEW BLOCKS AWAY FROM WHERE THE MASSES WERE PROTESTING against the Vietnam War and heralding the Free Speech Movement in Berkeley, California, one man was quietly planting the seeds for an American coffee revolution. On April 1, 1966, Alfred Peet opened his now legendary store on the corner of Vine and Walnut in north Berkeley, thus embarking on a mission to teach America the fine art of sourcing and roasting good coffee. It was not an espresso bar or a café, but simply a place whose irresistible aroma beckoned everyone in the neighborhood. Although Peet was not the only person seeking better coffee for America at the time, his cult following grew rapidly and had a long-lasting impact. Among those inspired by Peet were the founders of Starbucks who originally sold Peet's beans until Peet trained them in roasting, and George Howell who later brought good coffee to Boston and became one of the key figures in the specialty coffee industry in America.

Upon arriving in the United States a decade earlier, Alfred Peet was appalled to confirm American coffee's international reputation of tasting like dishwater. How such an advanced country could put up with such low quality coffee was beyond him. Peet started learning the fine art of coffee as a child when he worked in his father's coffee store in his native Netherlands. After World War II, Peet left the Netherlands and took the scenic route to the United States via the Dutch East Indies and New Zealand where he pursued tea, his other passion. Years later, Peet reconciled his two passions poetically: *"Tea is like a pair of ballet slippers; while coffee a pair of storm boots."*

As a superb cupper with deep knowledge of green beans, roasting and brewing equipment, and extensive relationships with coffee growers, Peet did not intend to open a café. He just wanted a space where he could educate his customers about the fine aspects of coffee and tea and sell his beans and leaves. In fact, he was quite annoyed by many of the characters that patronized his store. Lore has it that he even removed the few seats he had in the shop in the hopes of getting rid of the scruffy types. Alas, the floor proved to be adequate seating for his ardent fans. Alfred Peet is repeatedly described as an exacting man. He generously offered accolades for a job well done, but he did not suffer fools. When it came to providing constructive and gentle feedback, his interpersonal skills often failed him.

Peet sold his company in 1979 but remained its coffee buyer until 1983. Ironically, Jerry Baldwin, co-founder of Starbucks, Peets' roastmaster Jim Reynolds, and a few other investors bought Peet's in 1984. In 1987 Baldwin sold his share in Starbucks to focus on the Peet's chain. Baldwin and Howard Schultz, the new owner of Starbucks, signed a non-compete agreement that precluded Starbucks from opening stores in the San Francisco Bay Area for five years. Today, Peet's operates about 200 stores, mostly in California. Peet's original store, serving as an anchor to an area known as the "Gourmet Getto" that includes other famous establishments such as *Chez Panisse*, has been remodeled. It now houses a small museum that displays Peet's memorabilia, including his brewing and roasting equipment and letters from notable fans.

On the other side of the San Francisco Bay, a different kind of history was being made. Gianni Giotta opened Caffe Trieste in the North Beach neighbor-

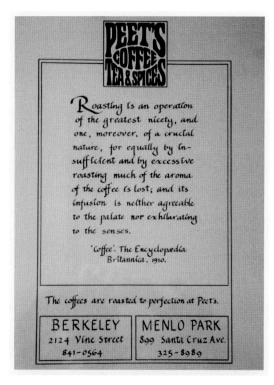

The gibraltar, the cult drink of San Francisco.

Caffe Trieste in San Francisco's North Beach neighborhood

hood of San Francisco in 1956, and introduced the first espresso machine west of the Mississippi River. Gianni named his café after the legendary Italian coffee city north of his home village whose cafés he fondly missed. His early customers were mostly the Italians living in the neighborhood. In due time, the relatively unassuming café became the place where San Franciscans learned to love a cappuccino (loving espresso would come only a few decades later). The café also became the center of social and literary activity in the city. As Andrew Barnett, a San Francisco coffee guru describes, *"When you enter Caffe Trieste, you can still feel the atmosphere where the leaders of the anti-conformist Beat Movement such as Jack Kerouac and Allen Ginsberg sat and discussed the issues of the day, or where Francis Ford Coppola wrote most of The Godfather scripts."* Indeed, Greg Sherwood, son of Don Sherwood the main spokesperson for the Beatniks, strongly attests to Barnett's observations every time he is greeted by old-timers at the café.

The center of coffee gravity shifted from San Francisco to the Pacific Northwest cities of Seattle and Portland during the 1980's and 1990's. Sporting a vibrant scene of specialty roasters and propelled by the fame of Starbucks, the northerners often looked down at the coffee scene in San Francisco. With the help of folks like Andrew Barnett, San Francisco swung back in the last decade and has now reclaimed its formidable stature on the American coffee scene.

Barnett was first exposed to espresso culture at Caffe Trieste as an art student at San Francisco State University, an experience that would change his career path a few years later. In 1994, he opened his first café in Santa Rosa, the largest town in the center of Sonoma Valley, one of California's famed wine producing regions. His hired pastry chef at the café was so good that somewhat to Barnett's chagrin, Western Caffe won the best new *restaurant* in Sonoma County award in 1995. Barnett was deeply influenced by the legendary David Schomer, founder of Espresso Vivace in Seattle whom he met in 1994 at a coffee show. Not only was Barnett smitten with the sweetest tasting Vivace espresso, he was also impressed by Schomer's highly principled and meticulous method for coffee-making and research. Barnett served Vivace beans for several years until he started to roast his own.

Since the foot traffic in Santa Rosa at the time could not sustain a café such as Western, Barnett closed the café and teamed up with the kitchen manager to open the more profitable Centro Espresso, an espresso cart in Santa Rosa. Between these two ventures, Barnett took a job as an assistant manager at a local Starbucks. His avid fans gave him a hard time during that period. They came to Starbucks demanding the same coffee quality

Andrew Barnett of Ecco Caffe

they had at Western Caffe. Barnett diplomatically punted by explaining to his customers that Starbucks offers a *"different expression"* of coffee. He actually claims that in experiments performed before opening hours, Vivace's coffee did not come out the same on Starbucks' equipment. Barnett started roasting his own beans in 2000 and founded Ecco Caffe to focus on roasting and sourcing coffees. He has become known worldwide for his superior cupping skills and served several times as a judge in the World Barista Championship. In 2009, Ecco was acquired by Intelligentsia Coffee, a leader in American specialty coffee.

The esteemed specialty coffee scene in San Francisco received a further boost in 2002 when James Freeman opened Blue Bottle Coffee, 319 years after its namesake opened in Vienna. Freeman describes himself as a *"slightly disaffected freelance musician and coffee lunatic, weary of the grande eggnog latte and the double skim pumpkin-pie macchiato."* Freeman opened Blue Bottle Coffee at the Berkeley Farmer's market, and later moved to the San Francisco Ferry Farmer's market where customers are willing to regularly spend 40 minutes in line for his coffee. Freeman's message is simple: coffee needs to be served fresh. When he started, he poured every cup individually and never served coffee that was roasted more than two days earlier.

Matthew Williams, a barista at Four Barrel Coffee. The café also served as the venue for celebrating Matthew's marriage to Zachary Carlsen, also a barista at Four Barrel, and co-founder of Sprudge.com, the site for coffee comic relief.

With its stellar cafés that offer top-notch quality coffees, San Francisco is staging a huge comeback. The comeback was further fueled by more help from the Pacific Northwest when Jeremy Tooker and Eileen Hassi came to San Francisco to work for a new branch of Tor-refazione Coffee, one of Seattle's beloved coffee establishments. When rumors that Starbucks might buy the chain started surfacing, the two joined forces to open their own café, thus giving birth to Ritual Coffee Roasters in the hip Mission District of San Francisco. Today, Ritual is home to Ben Kaminsky, the three-time coffee tasting champion of the United States. A bit later, Jeremy Tooker went on to start Four Barrel Coffee that is a few blocks up the road from Ritual on Valencia Street. Four Barrel, a beautifully designed café, is punctuated by an old world feel. In both cafés, you will find a broad selection of single-origin coffees from the best farms. Constantly springing up in the city are new cafés such as Sightglass that features its roasting machine front and center and Ma.Velous that is serving beans from top roasters from around the world. These cafés, like others in their class, spend significant effort in developing relationships with coffee growers and exporters so they have access to the best beans year after year. Together, they are cultivating a dazzling barista and coffee culture in the city that would make Alfred Peet proud.

Silicon Valley

San Francisco sits forty miles north of Silicon Valley, the world's technology mecca that is home to the headquarters of tech giants such as Google, Hewlett Packard, Apple, and Facebook. The casual café scene in Silicon Valley is characterized by gatherings of entrepreneurs, investors, and university faculty and students of all complexions and ethnic origins. Café Barrone in Menlo Park has long enjoyed the patronage of the Stanford community and Sand Hill Road venture capitalists. Café Venetia, Coupa Café, and others in downtown Palo Alto, as well as a bustling Philz Coffee branch in midtown Palo Alto and Barefoot Café in Santa Clara, each provides a different atmosphere that is conducive for cooking up the next startup, closing a crucial deal, or a meeting of top executives to discuss how to avert a collision between two tech titans. ✎

A skip and a hop from the venture capital epicenter of Sand Hill Road, Café Borrone in Menlo Park is a Silicon Valley institution known for tech-heavy meetings.

SEATTLE: Coffee Capital of the U.S.A

IT IS 7AM AND DAVID SCHOMER IS BIK-ING FROM HIS HOME in the Fremont neighborhood of Seattle to Espresso Vivace, a café that he founded in 1988. He is on a mission to solve a mystery to the benefit of his discerning coffee clientele: one of the group heads on the espresso machine is not producing perfect shots of espresso. After futzing around with the machine for a while, David discovered the reason: the water temperature in the group head was 2.5 Fahrenheit degrees lower than the optimal. When David says optimal, he knows what he is talking about. He had spent 15 years researching every requisite step in the making of a consummate espresso shot. His thorough research results reveal that the ideal brewing temperature for espresso is 203.5 degrees and should not vary by more than one degree during the brewing process. Having taken serious note of Schomer's research, high end manufacturers of

David Schomer futzing with an espresso machine.

espresso machines now produce machines with special temperature controllers that adhere to his exacting specifications. The scope of Schomer's research extends to the right type of water, grinding, dosing and tamping techniques, and brewing time. His famous "green book" entitled *Espresso Coffee* explains and illustrates his techniques in detail and is a staple on the shelves of many baristas around the world. His video on latte art is credited with popularizing latte art in the United States. Working from his small coffee company in Seattle, Schomer's methodologies have profoundly influenced and inspired baristas in the United States and beyond.

Seattle is considered by many to be the Coffee Capital of the United States. When asked why, most will probably point to the origins of Starbucks and assume that Seattle is essentially one big Starbucks café accented with the Space Needle. Seattle's coffee prominence was highlighted and reinforced by the TV series *Frasier* where the psychiatrist Frasier Crane typically sipped a latte in a Seattle café with his quirky brother as the next wave of trouble unfolded in their lives. While Seattle definitely has its fair share of Starbucks, it is the spirit of coffee artisans like David Schomer and the small yet distinctive cafés that they run that truly define the coffee culture in the Emerald City.

Schomer traces his fascination for all facets of coffee making to his first brushes with coffee as a child, when his mother let him smell the enticing aroma of freshly ground beans. When his parents finally allowed him to take a sip a few years later, he was profoundly disappointed by the bitter taste (the term *"burnt matches"* was the exact quote). Since then, his motto

Espresso Vivace

has been to *"make coffee taste as good as it smells."*

Schomer was trained in metrology, the science of measurements. He worked in the United States Airforce and then at the Boeing Company with instruments whose resolution was finer than one part per million. In parallel, he developed his passion for the flute. These two parts of his brain define his approach to coffee: an artisan informed by the scientific method. His espresso style is based on the northern Italian roast that develops the caramelized sugars within the bean to create a sweet flavor in the cup. In contrast, a southern Italian roast (often referred to as French Roast in the U.S.) is darker and often leaves more of the roasting flavor in the cup.

Schomer founded Espresso Vivace on Capitol Hill, the center of counter culture in Seattle and home to many artists and musicians. Capitol Hill is also home to other peer roasters such as Victrola and Vita. When he started out, Schomer planned to use the coffee business to support his flute avocation. But coffee quickly became his main passion. His musical training did serve him well though. Over the years, he has hired many musicians as baristas at Espresso Vivace. He claims that the best baristas are those who have some other artistic outlet in their lives. The several baristas at Vivace who have been with him for over 15 years are a testament to Schomer's successful philosophy: treating your baristas as artists at work makes them happy and more productive.

One of the people responsible for the ex-

The scene at Café Bauhaus on Capitol Hill.

Kent Bakke

acting standards and innovations demanded by Schomer is Kent Bakke, the current CEO of La Marzocco International, a manufacturer of high-end espresso machines. Bakke started his coffee career in 1977 when, *"There were eight espresso machines in Seattle and not all of them worked."* To a bunch of ex-hippies wondering what to do, opening a café seemed like a relatively easy task. Because Seattle was isolated from other cities that had any semblance of an espresso culture, its residents had no preconceived notions about what an espresso should be. With that competitive advantage, the early café pioneers set out to simply make things as good as they could be.

Bakke quickly realized that he was much more interested in tinkering around with espresso machines than running a café business. During a trip to Italy with his friends Asa Bron and Barbara Douma, the three came up with a business plan to import espresso machines from Italy. One of his suppliers was La Marzocco, a family owned business from Tuscany that later supplied machines to Starbucks. As Starbucks was embarking on a major expansion in 1994, Bakke inquired with La Marzocco about doubling their production. Because that idea did not sit well with the lifestyle embraced by the La Marzocco family, Bakke ended up buying the company and producing the machines in Seattle for Starbucks. In 2004, when Starbucks switched to more automated Swiss-made machines, the bulk of Bakke's production of La Marzocco was exported to Italy. As the chief of La Marzocco, Bakke constantly listens to the needs voiced by the likes of Schomer. As a result, their machines now have controllers called PIDs (Proportional, Integral and Derivative) that are capable of keeping the temperature steady within half a degree of the optimal.

Thanks to Kent Bakke, anyone unable to make it to a café in Seattle can have an espresso cart make its way to you. Together with his business partner John Blackwell and John's handy brother Jim, Bakke built the first espresso cart in 1978 and used it at the Edmunds Art Festival that year. After the festival, the cart came to downtown Seattle and became an instant hit that was widely copied and spread to other parts of the country. Espresso carts provide a relatively low cost way to start a business and make good use of spaces where full-sized cafés are difficult or impracticable to fit. Today, the city of Seattle is imposing much more stringent espresso cart permit requirements, resulting in many of the carts moving inside to complement other businesses.

Café Allegro in Seattle's University District: the venue of my first date with Oriana.

A question that may still linger on your mind is why did Seattle, of all U.S. cities, claim the title of Coffee Capital? An easy explanation (especially from the perspective of the slightly envious Californians) is that Seattle resident's take up additional doses of caffeine to cope with the rainy and cloudy weather. Seattlites' high level of caffeine consumption has recently been backed up by an unexpected source: a 2000 survey of the sewage system in Seattle revealed elevated levels of caffeine. Another explanation for Seattle's reputation is that the city has a large Scandinavian community whose members are known for their high coffee standards. Others have explained that wealthy Microsoft employees and other members of the thriving technopreneur community in Seattle have money to spend and cook up their best ideas over $4 plus lattes.

Schomer resolves the mystery in more artful terms. People come to Seattle for its beauty and outdoor opportunities (the "Rainier factor"). The independent and creative spirit of Seattlites has enabled the formation of deep subcultures in diverse areas such as chess, music and pool. These folks who have a fine appreciation for both aesthetics and substance are naturally drawn to the masterful artisanship and sophisticated tastes of good coffee. These unsettled conjectures aside, there is no doubt that the commitment of Schomer, Bakke and their partners to high quality espresso was a major force in pushing the quality of coffee in the United States up more than a few notches. ✍

PORTLAND: The Rival Coffee Capital

IN ADDITION TO SEATTLE, PORTLAND ALSO CLAIMS THE TITLE COFFEE CAPITAL OF THE UNITED STATES. It may have an argument in its favor: a city that is on the way from San Francisco to Seattle was bound to get caught up in the coffee crossfire. Moreover, Portland enjoys the Pacific Northwest weather that draws people to extra doses of caffeine and a laid-back and free-spirited atmosphere where coffee artisans thrive. Unlike its better known neighbor to the north, Portland has a feature that is attractive to coffee professionals—affordable housing.

The big break that elevated Portland's coffee to the national stage came from Duane Sorenson, a native of Puyallup, Washington. Sorenson opened up Stumptown Coffee Roasters in 1999 and has built it into a top-tier third wave coffee establishment. Sorenson and his green coffee buyer Aleco Chigounis scour the world looking for the best coffee lots they can find and pay whatever price is needed to acquire them. Reputed for being driven by Sorenson's passion and not always by business considerations, Stumptown has expanded from Portland to Seattle and New York. Since Sorenson has a particular fascination with Amsterdam, he even opened up a temporary café there in the summer of 2010. The coffee scene in Portland is expanding rapidly with many other micro-roasteries springing up and pursuing coffee excellence on similar albeit smaller scales as the acclaimed Stumptown. 🍂

Water Avenue Coffee Company in southeast Portland

Duane Sorenson of Stumptown Coffee Roasters

STARBUCKS: The Coffee Giant

COFFEE LOVERS' REACTIONS TO STARBUCKS SPAN THE GAMUT OF COFFEE EMOTIONS. To some, Starbucks is synonymous with coffee culture. To others, the mere mention of the world's largest coffeehouse chain triggers a tirade of mockery. Starbucks is so pervasive that many people cannot even name its closest competitor or fathom that for some neighborhoods, Starbucks remains a distant dream to be materialized. So what is the role of Starbucks in shaping today's coffee culture? What makes this ubiquitous company at once a revered success story and frequent target of ridicule?

To understand the Starbucks phenomenon, one needs to keep in mind the coffee scene before Starbucks entered. Coffee quality was pretty bad in most parts of America. Coffeehouses were very few and far in between. Much of the coffee was consumed in diners where the ambiance left much to be desired. After visiting the lively café scene of Italy in the early 1980's, Howard Schultz, the human locomotive that has been driving Starbucks since 1987, crystallized his vision to adapt that type of spirited café experience to America. Today, with over 11,000 cafés in the U.S. alone, Starbucks provides a pleasant, highly accessible, and informal place for a social meeting, an informal job interview, or a first date with no strings attached.

In one of its earlier strokes of marketing genius, Starbucks came up with a colorful ordering vocabulary that enabled customers to exercise their imagination to create customized drinks of their choice. For example, you may start with a simple double tall wet half-caf cappuccino, then move on to the grande, non-fat, sugar-free cinnamon dolce latte, no whip. The single-tall-non-decaf-latte, a.k.a. a *"why bother"* may set you back a few bucks, but should keep your waistline thin. The ability to control your own coffee destiny with these customized orders has been a highly prized Starbucks attribute that has not gone unnoticed by Hollywood. Starbucks lingo made its way into the cinematic hall of fame when Steve Martin's character in *L.A. Story* asked for a *"half double decaffeinated half-caf with a twist of lemon"* at Café L'Idiot.

Another notable characteristic of Starbucks is its willingness to go the extra mile on customer convenience. Starbucks cafés are strategically located in high foot traffic areas so you can enjoy a cup of coffee on your way to and from work, school, or the gym. Is crossing the street too much of a setback to your morning routine? No problem! Starbucks will open another branch to save you the crossing. In 1999, after a particular Starbucks in Portland, Maine had its windows shattered by vandals several weekends in a row, Conan O'Brien quipped on his late night comedy show that customers were com-

Long line at the original Pike Place Starbucks

Coffee beans for Starbucks being dried at J. Hill Mill in Santa Ana, El Salvador.

plaining because *"for several weeks now, they've had to use the Starbucks across the street."*

So what's wrong then? As Taylor Clark describes in his book *Starbucked: A Double Tall Tale of Caffeine, Commerce, and Culture,* complaints against Starbucks fall into several categories. Coffee quality tops the list. Starbucks' roast is darker than the darkest Italian roast and has been dubbed "Charbucks." According to experts, the benefit of dark roasts is that unlike lighter roasts, the coffee may still be tasted even after generous pours of milk and other additives are in the drink. Notwithstanding this quality issue, even the professionals

Starbucks in Shanghai

will admit that when stranded at an airport or in a foreign city without their usual coffee bearings, any Starbucks will offer them at least something predictable.

The skills of the Starbucks baristas have been nose-diving. Most of the preparation today has become highly automated, so much so that the baristas need only press the right buttons and make sure the milk is steamed to satisfy the sensor readings. The minimal training required to become a Starbucks barista was brought to light by an event that happened on April 30, 2002 at 5am, when two robbers targeted a Starbucks drive-by shop in the city of Monroe, Washington. The robbers were unsatisfied with the amount of cash the store carried at that hour and decided to increase their loot by tapping directly into the revenue stream. After locking up the baristas in the back room, they started serving drinks themselves for about half an hour. The robbers fled the scene before anyone could complain about the quality of the drinks.

Another major source of complaint against Starbucks stems from the wider fear of gentrification whereby the big chains including McDonald's and Walmart have displaced the mom and pop shops and caused cities and communities to lose their distinctive characters. Starbucks does not come into a community with a whisper. It will typically open several stores, even five to ten, in its initial assault on a metropolitan area and always finds some canny way to make a grand entrance. As a result of their clustering and other practices, many local coffee shops have been forced to go out of business.

Starbucks goes to great lengths to secure the retail spaces they most desire. When one of Starbucks' real estate dealers, Tracy Cornell, was trying to close a transaction on a particularly attractive location in San Francisco, the landlord (who apparently was not a big fan of Starbucks) refused to even meet with her. Unfazed, Cornell's sleuthing revealed that the landlord was a physician. She proceeded to schedule an appointment with him pretending to be a patient. By the end of the appointment, the deal was cinched with no medication prescribed.

While the onslaught of Starbucks has forced the closure of many local coffee shops, some point out that Starbucks' arrival often provides excellent opportunities for the well-prepared cafépreneurs. In fact, some go as far as suggesting that aspiring cafépreneurs follow Starbucks when scouting out golden locations to open a coffee shop because the giant will have already performed a thorough feasibility analysis. Further, customers will start scoping out other coffee shops once they realize that the frappuccino is not the ultimate coffee drink this planet has to offer. Essentially, Starbucks' role is to pique the community's interest in exploring good coffee. Beyond that, there is plenty of room for local innovation and more nuanced coffee experiences. The key challenge for independent cafés in these communities is to carve out a distinctive niche rather than imitate standardized Starbucks. ✎

COFFEE COWBOYS & EVANGELISTS

ALFRED PEET LAUNCHED THE COFFEE REVOLU-
TION in the United States and helped propel the
reputation of American coffee beyond dishwater.
His followers built the Starbucks empire that has
become the symbol of American coffee. While
Peet's and Starbucks exemplify second wave coffee establishments, in the past 15 years the United
States and worldwide specialty coffee industry has
gone through yet another revolution. The third
wave is led by cowboys who travel to the ends of
the earth in search of the best beans and evan-
gelists who spare no effort to bring outstanding
coffees to the American consumer.

"*This generation is in love with the coffee,*" explains George Howell, a household name in the
specialty coffee industry. "*Before them, coffee quality was pursued to a point, but it was ultimately about
the business. These guys are obsessed about the coffee
and take incredible risks in pursuit of the best quality.*" Now in his mid-60's, Howell is a father of six
and a professor at heart who can spew a stream
of pithy quotes at a drop of a hat. He speaks with
commanding authority from a career that spans
the entire history of specialty coffee in the United
States. The roots of Howell's career go back to
Berkeley in the 1960's, to the revolution started by
Alfred Peet. While Howell was not a fan of Peet's
dark roast, he was inspired by the atmosphere
and excitement at Peet's café. When he returned
to the East Coast in 1974 with the intention of re-
suming his studies at Yale University, he became
distraught over bad coffee that tasted like "*wooden
pellets*" and decided to help spread Peet's revolu-
tionary fervor by starting the Coffee Connection
in the heart of Harvard Square.

The first Coffee Connection store was opened in
a building that dates back to the early 1900's and
even had a ramp that was designed for the horse
and buggy. Though his roastery was not co-located
with the café, the new standards Howell was trying to set required that he find a way to underscore
the freshness of his coffee. In a rather innovative

Above: George Howell in the middle. On the left, his daughter Jenny Howell who is the Director
of Coffee at Terroir Coffee, Howell's newest venture. On the right, Maria Santos Montilla Cerón,
a farmer from the mountains of Cauca, Colombia. A widow, Maria has grown and harvested coffee for many years with the help of one permanent employee and her daughter.

move for the period, he posted the roasting dates on the coffee barrels. At the time, Howell was also immersed in the arts and jazz scene.
Having spent some of his formative years in Mexico City, he was particularly fascinated by folk art. He lamented the fact that the folk
artists were trapped in a system that insisted on and reinforced their anonymity. Despite Howell's numerous attempts to convince them
otherwise, the local art experts and educators did not see a path out of this conundrum. Opening his first store in Harvard Square was

a way of setting up a showroom for these artists on the doorstep of an intellectual mecca that is Harvard University. A quarter of a century later, a different set of anonymous artists weighed heavily on Howell's mind as he organized the Cup of Excellence to help recognize the individual coffee farmers as first class citizens and integrate them into the full chain of coffee celebrations.

Between 1974 and 1994, Howell grew the Coffee Connection to 24 stores (mostly in the Boston area but some as far as New Jersey). As the region's leading chain, the Coffee Connection became a natural acquisition target for Starbucks as it sought rapid national expansion in the early 90's. The Boston media was in a tizzy as confrontation between the Coffee Goliath and the local favorite heated up. Howell recalls that at the height of the frenzy, photos showing him with a white-lined moustache ready to battle Starbucks with his own lattes were plastered all over the Boston subways. That cinched his decision to sell the Coffee Connection to Starbucks in 1994: *"I knew it wasn't about the coffee anymore, but about advertising."*

Like other coffee companies at the time, the Coffee Connection purchased their beans from a small number of coffee importers. These importers had a limited selection of coffees from each origin and the roasters had little if any knowledge of how their coffees were processed. Only much later did roasters get into the business of selecting their coffees by cupping. George Howell was in the coffee business for an entire 13 years before he cupped coffee for the first time! His first cup-

Intelligentsia Coffee in Silver Lake, Los Angeles.

Geoff Watts cupping at the 2011 Cup of Excellence judging in Colombia.

ping experience took place in 1988 in Costa Rica where he was given five coffees and asked to choose the best. He had a very different experience in Kenya shortly thereafter, where the Kenyans were cupping 400 coffees a week and then selling the coffees in an auction based on their respective grades. His frequent visits to farms in Kenya and Costa Rica enabled him to feature beans from individual coops and farms and planted the seeds of the third wave. This contribution was acknowledged in 1996 by a Lifetime Achievement Award presented to him from the Specialty Coffee Association of America.

Several companies entered the specialty coffee market in the mid to late 1990's, fully bringing on the third wave that generally refers to the *"in love with the coffee"* generation alluded to by Howell. Most notable among these are Intelligentsia Coffee and Tea from Chicago, Stumptown from Portland, Oregon, and Counter Culture from Durham, North Carolina. These companies and their peers have fundamentally changed the way coffee is sourced and served in the United States. Geoff Watts, the Director of Coffee at Intelligentsia, lamented his frustration at the limited choices he was offered by his importers and his inability to influence the processing of coffee. For example, he had access to merely five different coffees from Guatemala even though the country had hundreds of farms that produced a variety of distinctive coffees.

Watts and his peers resorted to what can best described as rugged American individualism (a.k.a. cowboy attitude) to pioneer a new approach to sourcing coffee. They started traveling to origin and literally knocking on farmers' doors looking for good coffee. To find interesting farms, they took whatever lead they could corral, whether it was from local coffee exporters, regional coffee competitions, or non-government organizations in the area.

They started close to home in Central America and brushed up on their Spanish while on the move. At first, Watts only knew what flavor profiles he was looking for, but nothing about how these profiles were affected by the processing that took place on the farms. He wanted to form direct and long-term relationships with farmers. However, there were so many variables to consider when choosing which farms to work with, such as the region, climate, soil, and varietals. He decided to go with the one variable he felt confident assessing: the human variable. He forged relationships with farmers with whom he shared chemistry and a common vision.

As the breadth and depth of their experiences grew, Watts and his peers were able to offer advice to farmers on how to improve the quality of their coffee. The advice was sometimes as simple as picking the cherries only when they were ripe, making certain that the water they were being fermented in was clean, and raking the beans on the drying patios to ensure even drying. In many cases this was not news to the farmers. However, they had no financial incentive to improve their practices. Watts and his colleagues decided to pay farmers markedly higher prices in order to put the right incentives in place and change attitudes. As the coffee cowboys traveled the world, they transferred

From seed ...

To cup.

coffee processing techniques across oceans. For example, fermentation methods that had been used for generations in Kenya started being applied in Honduras thereby improving the quality of the latter's coffee.

To be clear, the so-called direct trade and the relationships forged are not an exclusively American trend. The Europeans, Japanese, Koreans and Australians have been traveling and forging direct relationships with farmers as well. The difference is that the Americans typi-

The founding team of Handsome Coffee Roasters in L.A.

cally have deeper pockets and their proximity to the main coffee growing regions of the world facilitates their travel.

Back at home, multiple changes were taking place at cafés all over the United States. Alternatives to Starbucks that served a variety of single-origin coffees in addition to artisan blends were mushrooming everywhere. The Roasters' Guild of America was founded in 2000 to provide roasters venues for learning and exchanging ideas. In 2003, the Barista Guild of America was formed to provide an organization for a profession that had been considered as a fleeting occupation for college students. Doug Zell, the founder of Intelligentsia, was particularly passionate about fostering a barista culture that enticed the best in the field. From the very start he wanted to create a dynamic culture in which baristas not only survive, but rather, thrive and have the opportunity to continuously improve and refine their craft.

It was this rapidly evolving culture that beckoned Mike Phillips in 2006. Mike had the typical qualifications of an aspiring barista: a degree in digital art, experience selling vacuum cleaners and slinging pizzas, and a passion for dancing. He is also a total goofball considered by all to be the nicest guy imaginable. He had been a home barista geek for a few years when he was introduced to Doug Zell at the Great Lakes Barista Championship in 2006. He recalls how flabbergasted he was that Zell recognized his screen name from the Coffee Geek web site. Mike took an entry position at Intelligentsia, blending and packing coffee at Roaster Works in Chicago. Gradually but surely, he made his way up to bar-back (side-kicks for baristas), certified Intelligentsia barista, and in-store educator.

Then came 2009. Placing fifth at the Great Lakes Regional Barista Championship did not earn Mike a trip to the U.S. Barista Championship in Portland Oregon. Determined to press on, he asked Doug Zell for permission to pay his own way. In Portland, Mike shocked the barista world by winning the championship title. Second and third places also went to Intelligentsia baristas.

After placing third at the 2009 World Barista Championship in Atlanta, Mike wanted to take a reprieve from competitions. He changed his mind after a February 2010 visit to the Coope Dota farming collective in Costa Rica. Blown away by the variety of the collective's processing methods, he was inspired to execute on an idea he had several years earlier: to design a routine that illustrates how processing methods affect taste profiles. After recapturing the United States Barista Championship he qualified to take another shot at the world title in London. To add a little stress to the situation, Mike broke his pinkie playing frisbee a few weeks before the June 2010 WBC. Unfazed and as determined as ever, Mike gave his best and performed flawlessly in London. A mere four years after embarking on his coffee career, Mike became the first American to be crowned World Barista Champion. A year later, Mike and a couple of his colleagues founded Handsome Coffee Roasters in Los Angeles to continue the pursuit of their own version of coffee passion. ✍

THE AMERICAN MIDWEST

SURROUNDED BY CORNFIELDS AS FAR AS THE EYE CAN SEE, West Lafayette, Indiana, the home of Purdue University and not much else, sits in the heart of the American Midwest. This is most certainly not a place awaiting the new waves of the coffee industry. Twenty years ago, when Ahmed Alsoffi arrived here from Yemen for Business School and Ahmed Elmagarmid from Libya arrived to start his computer science career, they realized the severity of the situation and took matters into their own hands.

The two Ahmeds started the café of their fantasies and called it Café Vienna to invoke thoughts of grandeur and culture in their patronage. They sourced the best coffee beans they could find and served the most tempting pastries (even if the cost was ridiculous at the time). Over time, Elmagarmid shifted his focus to his scientific career while Alsoffi became the busiest businessman in town who opened several cafés and restaurants. His most recent venture, Café Royale, still serves as the morning meeting spot for their cohort. In addition to the excellent coffees and eats at the café, the main attraction is the coffee-themed restrooms that are beautifully designed and decorated by local artists. ✎

NEW YORK CITY: The Café Bazaar

THE COFFEE SCENE IN COSMOPOLITAN NEW YORK IS A CONSTANTLY EVOLVING ONE. Even though New York City has been home to the first espresso machine in the United States since 1927, it never developed its own nationally known coffee establishment. The reason is simple—it does not have to. To entice the sophisticated palates of New Yorkers, every coffee company yearns to open up shop in the Big Apple. From Stumptown Coffee that set up shop in the Ace Hotel, Intelligentsia that opened a lab in the city and serves its coffee in several cafés, to the local chain Joe's Coffee that is serving coffee roasted by San Francisco coffee guru Andrew Barnett, everyone is vying for a slice of this gigantic melting pie.

Exorbitant real estate prices in New York preclude large café spaces. Hole-in-the-wall cafés like Abraço Café are very typical. Fortunately, ample seating is not always a requirement for always-on-the-go New Yorkers. ✎

Coffee themed decor in the bathroom of Café Royale in West Lafayette, Indiana

Hole-in-the-wall Abraço Café in New York City

SOUTH & CENTRAL AMERICA

South and Central America are home to about two thirds of the world's coffee production. Brazil leads with half that number. The region's coffee farms are endowed with the topographical advantages of high altitude and special volcanic soils that enable the cultivation of some of the world's most prized coffees. The history of coffee offers powerful insights into the social strifes that have so often plagued the young nations and the deep cultural divide between the European settlers and the indigenous population.

The arrival of coffee to this region is not without its enthralling stories. French army captain Gabriel de Clieu is credited with clandestinely transporting a coffee plant from Paris across the Atlantic Ocean in 1723 and heroically protecting it against every imaginable threat along the way. Bringing coffee to Brazil required the skills and finesse of a Brazilian mediator who was determined to import coffee into his country at any cost.

Much has been written about the coffee production in this part of the world. In the next few chapters we focus on an exciting recent phenomenon, the fruitful cross-fertilization between the production and consumption sides of coffee that is taking place throughout the region. While producers are gaining more knowledge about cupping and consumer desires, baristas and roasters are benefiting from having coffee farms within driving distance. In Guatemala we visit two representative farms, guided by Raul Rodas who made history in 2010 by becoming the first barista from a producing country to advance to the finals of the World Barista Championship. Since his second place finish, Raul has become a role model to whom baristas in the entire region look up. In Costa Rica we visit Coope Dota, a 50-year-old coffee cooperative whose list of buyers includes the best-known labels in the industry. In addition to producing world-class coffee, the cooperative trains roasters and baristas and has even developed a high school curriculum around coffee. In El Salvador we spend time with trailblazing Aida Batlle, a fifth generation coffee farmer who returned to her home country after the civil war necessitated an absence of 24 years.

Hands down, Colombia wins the award for best coffee marketing. Its masterful representation of the country's fine coffees through the fictitious character of an affable and humble farmer named Juan Valdez has created not only a widely recognized icon but also an enduring aura of mystique that reinforces the perception of Colombian coffee as among the most accessible, highest quality, and most admired in the world. In Brazil, the world's leading producer and second largest consumer of coffee, we witness both a grand scale pursuit of excellence in coffee production and a burgeoning café culture whose level of sophistication is gradually catching up with the reputation of its coffees.

Coffee farmer on a drying patio that overlooks the Quindio region of Colombia.

GUATEMALA: Sublime Coffees from the Volcanic Slopes

ON APRIL 15, 2009 THE EVE OF THE WORLD BARISTA CHAMPIONSHIP in Atlanta, Raul Rodas the Barista Champion of Guatemala faced a wrenching decision: to use the coffee beans that his company supplied him for the competition or the coffee with which he had fallen in love. Both coffees were from Guatemala, though his true love had reached Atlanta clandestinely via a concerted international effort of coffee professionals. Using his beloved beans could cost him his job, but his heart told him that those superior beans would better showcase Guatemala's coffee excellence.

A few months earlier, Raul had tasted coffee grown on the Finca La Maravilla, a farm in the Huehuetenango region of northern Guatemala, a few miles away from the Mexican border. He was introduced to these beans by his colleagues from Intelligentsia Coffee and Tea in Chicago. Because his company did not source from this farm, using the La Maravilla beans to compete was out of the question. His company tried to find beans that would replicate the flavor, but to no avail. In parallel, Raul pursued Plan B. With the help of a friend, he managed to get the La Maravilla beans exported to the United States. Upon reaching the U.S., they were roasted especially for the competition by Intelligentsia in Chicago, who also drove the beans down to Atlanta together with those of the U.S. barista champion. Since Raul

Raul Rodas performing at the 2010 World Barista Championship in London

was sharing a hotel room with his manager at the time, the beans from La Maravilla were hidden in the room of his brother and sister who had come to Atlanta to support him.

After deliberating the decision for a few days, Raul followed his heart and donated his company-supplied beans to the hotel staff. To keep his secret, he had to be somewhat vague about the source of his beans during his presentation at the Championship. He came in 7th in the world, a very respectable position that fell just short of the six finalists.

Even though Raul lost his job when the truth came out, the event pushed the strong-minded and highly motivated young man to the next level of coffee excellence. In the year that followed, Raul used his new-found freedom to start his own exploration of Guatemalan coffees. He discovered a beautiful Geisha varietal in his country with which he recaptured the Guatemala barista championship for the third consecutive year. All of his efforts paid off when Raul made history at the 2010 WBC in London—he won second place, far better than any competitor from a coffee growing country had ever done. Raul has since been considered an inspiration to baristas throughout the coffee growing regions of the world.

Raul recounted his stories as we huddled around a bonfire on a chilly evening at the Finca La Maravilla. We arrived at the farm after a seven hour drive from Guatemala

Finca La Maravilla in the morning hours

City. During the last hour, we had to switch to a turbo engine powered pickup truck that was able to navigate the steep and serpentine path up the mountain.

La Maravilla started producing coffee in 2006 and yields about 600-800 60kg bags a year. It is nestled between two mountains in an unusual orientation that receives direct sunlight only in the morning hours. The afternoon shade is key to the ripening process during which sugars develop more thoroughly in the coffee cherries, yielding highly sought-after flavor profiles.

La Maravilla sprinted to greatness very quickly when it started selling to customers such as Intelligentsia Coffee and Sweet Maria's, a green coffee importer from Oakland, California. Distinguishing oneself from other farms in this region is quite a feat because the Huehuetenango is home to well-known labels such as Vista Hermosa and El Injerto (the latter holds the record for the highest price fetched in an Internet coffee auction of the Cup of Excellence—$80 per pound in 2008).

With its long tradition of estate coffee farming, diverse microregions, and high coffee quality stemming from advantageous altitude and technical processing expertise, Guatemala has always been a shining star within the specialty coffee community. It is also a country unique in Central America for its large indigenous population of Mayan descent.

Driving around the coffee farms in the Huehuetenango region, one cannot help but notice many signs of the country's deep social divide. In some places, the roads are lined with tiny drying patios for coffee. Behind the patios, it is not unusual to see family members de-pulp by hand the cher-

An indigenous Guatemalan picking cherries at the La Maravilla.

A café in Antigua

Enio and Raul Perez with the documents describing the lands owned by their families over the generations.

ries they harvested from their tiny farms. These families belong to the indigenous population that forms the majority in Guatemala. They speak their own languages and maintain their own strong cultures. Many of them do not have the means or know-how to process or transport their harvest to the local mills. They thus fall easy prey to "coyotes," individuals who roam the towns looking for fresh harvest, purchase them at low prices, and sell them for a profit to the mills that export the coffee. Mauricio Rosales, owner of La Maravilla and general manager of an exporting mill, claims that close to 60% of the coffee they process comes through coyotes.

Unlike the farmers of European descent who regard the land in utilitarian terms as a source of produce and income generator, the indigenous farmers view the land in more spiritual terms. Because they are thus reluctant to change their traditional ways of cultivating their lands, their lots yield much lower production and quality. Over the years, the government of Guatemala has instituted various programs aimed to introduce modern processing methods to these farmers. However, the initiatives have typically failed. Even a simple idea like using an alternative heating source has been met with resistance—lugging around packs of wood (mostly by women) is a time-honored part of their culture that they do not want to give up.

For a satisfying taste of the living history of Guatemalan coffee farming, Raul and I visited Finca La Soledad in the Acatemango Region of Guatemala. Situated in a valley between two volcanoes, it is only an hour away from the historic city of Antigua. Until as recently as 2006 when Acatemango gained its "coffee independence" with explicit recognition from Anacafé, the organization that oversees and administrates the Guatemalan coffee industry, Acatemango did not enjoy the same level of recognition in the coffee world as the celebrated coffee growing region of Antigua. Not surprisingly then, much of the coffee farmed in Acatenango had actually been transported to Antigua and relabeled in an effort to obtain premium prices associated with that region.

A family depulping coffee from their farm along the road in Huehuetenango, Guatemala

The arrival of coffee in Guatemala around 1870 coincided with the purchase by the great-great-grandfather of Enio Perez, the owner of La Soledad, of 900 hectares of land from a Spanish nobleman. The Perez family started growing coffee in 1895 and has been passing the farm on from one generation to the next. Over the years, the lots have been subdivided into smaller and smaller farms. After Enio doubled his farm by buying the land of one of his eleven siblings, Finca La Soledad stands at 90 hectares today. Amusingly, twelve of the thirteen members of the local coffee organization are from the Perez clan.

The unique quality of the coffee from La Soledad is attributable not only to the rich volcanic soil, the special microclimate, and the favorable altitudes (1740-1860 meters) at which the coffee is grown, but also the Perez family's great care and dedication to their profession. They have been making investments consistently over the years to advance quality and to become a standard-setter for social and environmental responsibility. Their unwavering commitment to quality has earned them several awards in the Cup of Excellence competitions in Guatemala, through which they became acquainted with some of their most esteemed customers including Intelligentsia Coffee, Sweet Maria's, and the George Howell Coffee Company. The family also invests heavily in their workforce by providing food supplies and encouraging pickers to send their children to elementary and high school.

The Perez family's history is intertwined with the history of Guatemala. During the Guatemalan civil war that lasted from 1960 until 1996, both the army and the opposing guerrillas came to the farm seeking help with food and clothing. The family tried very hard to remain neutral and treaded these landmines carefully lest aiding one side raised the ire of the other. Unfortunately, not everyone on the farm survived unscathed during those tumultuous years. Several of their workers, including the farm manager at the time, had disappeared without a trace.

One of La Soledad's critical success factors is its having mastered the art of cupping its own coffees. As demand for its specialty beans increased, Enio's son Raul decided that he would like to be more conversant with his buyers about the different attributes of his coffees. He started by attending cupping training from Anacafé. After Raul became a certified judge for the national barista competitions, he met Raul Rodas and their friendship began.

Sipping La Soledad coffee at the farm with both Rauls and watching Raul the farmer and Raul the barista enthusiastically discuss the fine aspects of growing and preparing coffee afforded a priceless vista of the current coffee ecosystem and culture of Guatemala. ✍

COSTA RICA: Coffee from *"a place high in the mountains that only birds can reach"*

WHEN MIKE PHILLIPS SHOWCASED THREE DIF-FERENT COFFEES in the presentation that earned him the 2010 World Barista Champion title in London, he was bringing to life the work of an entire community in the Dota Valley of Costa Rica. This is a farming community that is not only pursuing excellence and innovation in all steps of coffee production and preparation but at the same time, treasuring a rich family and community life.

Coope Dota is a cooperative of coffee farmers in the Tarrazu Region of Costa Rica, about a two hour drive south of the capital, San Jose. Though coffees are grown in all of Tarrazu and in several other regions of Costa Rica, the coffees grown in

The central square of Santa Maria with brightly dressed Panamanian workers relaxing by the monument of the revolution.

the Dota Valley have a special reputation for quality. They are grown at altitudes of 1,500-2,000 meters above sea level and are highly regarded for their chocolaty sweet notes and citrus flavors. Dota was the name of a local Indian chief. However, the Huetar Tribe that spent much of its time traversing this beautiful region used the word *"dota"* to mean *"a place high in the mountains that only birds can reach."*

The community is centered around the small town of Santa Maria, home to 3,500 people for most of the year. Even though downtown Santa Maria consists literally of one square block, that block has a revered place in the history of Costa Rica. It was here that a Dota coffee farmer named Jose Figueres Ferrer started the 1948 revolution against the military regime that had held a grip on the country. After escaping his farm fearing revenge by the military, Figueres had taken refuge right next to the city's central square. He hid there for a week as his supporters regained steam to move toward the capital and take over the country. Figueres was later elected to serve as the president of Costa Rica for three (non-consecutive) terms. Notably, he abolished the army during his first term.

The co-op, which celebrated its 50th anniversary in 2010 with great fanfare and with Mike Phillips as a guest of honor, is responsible for 90% of the economy of Santa Maria. Among other things, this means the co-op bankrolls the seniors' home and students in the local high school have a unique choice to major in coffee for their technical degree (in addition to the more common options of tourism, computer science or accounting). Students in the coffee major attend 500 hours of instruction over two years. The curriculum covers topics ranging from growing and processing coffee, to roasting, preparing and marketing. In the six years that the coffee study track has been offered, the high school has graduated about 15 to 20 students with this specialty every year. Some of the graduates have gone on to win titles at the Costa Rica Barista Championship. Competitors representing Coope Dota have always taken at least second or third place in the national barista championships, and in 2008 and 2009 they won the national title. In fact, they swept up the top three positions in 2009.

The co-op consists of 800 individual farmers (called associates) whose average farm size is two hectares. Collectively, the co-op produces 40,000 60kg bags of coffee per year, accounting for 10% of the annual coffee production in the Tarrazu Region. The co-op's buyers include leading labels such as Starbucks, Peet's, Tully's and high-end roasters such as Intelligentsia, the company for which Mike Phillips worked.

The associates of the co-op elect a board of directors who in turn appoints the general manager. In November 1994, the board appointed Roberto Mata as the general manager. And it has never looked back. Roberto's earlier non-farming ventures were severely disrupted twice by hurricanes. One of the hurricanes almost took his life as he was swept up in the river currents. Miraculously, he survived by having managed to cling to a tree branch. When driving through Santa Maria with Roberto, he waves to every passing car and stops for discussions with anyone who needs his attention. As the youngest of 13 children, father of five, and grandfather of eight, Roberto is a family man par excellence. Mike Phillips has poignantly described Roberto as *"the captain of the football team, the mayor and everyone's personal best friend, all rolled into one humble package."*

Roberto embarked on a "seed to cup" mission after experiencing an embarrassment of sorts during his first hosting occasion as general manager. He was mortified when his office assistant was about to serve visitors packaged coffee from the local supermarket!

Roberto Mata, the general manager of Coope Dota since 1994

That seemed utterly inconsistent with the image of a high-end coffee production enterprise he was trying to create. In response, Roberto strengthened his resolve to build in-house expertise in coffee preparation. He started a roastery alongside the processing plant. A few years later, he completed the "seed to cup" path by building a café and a strong barista training program. Visitors to Santa Maria today have the luxury of stopping by a café and having drinks prepared by award-winning baristas.

During the November to February coffee harvest season when children are out of school and temporary workers flood in from Nicaragua and Panama, Santa Maria's population doubles and the region becomes ever more colorful. Younger children have a blast playing in the fields as coffee is being picked, while those over 10 years old start helping their parents with the picking. Traditionally, Costa Rica was known in Central

Depulped coffee beans on the way to the washing process

Pickers bringing their harvest to the farm owner and counting their bounty.

America as a place where the farm owners worked the land and where a relatively egalitarian social structure emerged around coffee. However, the cost of Costa Rican labor has risen significantly in the last 15 years. Consequently, as the locals aspire for greater educational and professional pursuits, the laboring oar of most of the picking end up being taken by temporary workers. For the Nicaraguans who can pick coffee in their own country during the same period, the attraction of Costa Rica lies in the much higher pay—workers may earn up to four times more money. The Panamanians who come to pick coffee cherries in Costa Rica are mostly members of indigenous tribes, many of whom live in the remote jungles of northern Panama. Remote in this case means that to travel back home they need to take a bus from Costa Rica for two days, and from the bus stop they need to walk for three days in the jungle until they reach home.

The Panamanians in their eye-catching traditional garb are very noticeable in town when they fill up the streets during their off hours. On the weekends, their passion (some would say craze) for soccer takes over as they congregate on the soccer field in the center of town. The locals are understanding and enjoy other sports during that period. During their sojourn in Costa Rica, the Panamanians also occupy the resources of the medical clinics. One of the interesting cultural differences that the Costa Rican coffee farm owners learned when they proposed to build a daycare center for the workers is that their guests would never imagine leaving their children with anyone else. For them, their kids are their greatest treasures and they must take personal responsibility for every aspect of their care.

On a typical harvest day, the co-op bustles with a succession of farmers arriving in their pickup trucks to deposit their freshly picked coffee cherries. On the spot, the volume of the coffee is measured in boxes called *cahuelas*. Immediately after the weighing, farmers are given a receipt for the crop that may be taken directly to the bank to cash out.

Coope Dota uses a variety of methods to process its bountiful coffee cherries. In fact, Mike Phillips had requested the co-op to process his cherries using three different methods so he can demonstrate to the WBC judges how the taste of the resulting cup changes drastically. Under one method, known as natural processing, the complete cherry is dried in the sun before the bean is separated from the husk. At the other extreme, called fully washed, the cherry is first depulped and then washed thoroughly to remove the mucilage (the sweet honey-like substance that covers the bean's husk) before it is put to dry. An intermediate method, called honey processing, removes the skin from the cherry but lets it dry with the pulp and mucilage intact. The washed coffee produces a crisper cup, while the others retain more of the sweetness in the bean. Creating these coffees is made possible by the co-op's micro mill that enables them to process specific high quality lots separately and then sell them individually for higher prices. Micro mills arose in response to the traditional mode of processing coffee in Costa Rica where all the lots were lumped together and there was only a very coarse distinction among different coffee qualities.

In today's market where coffee prices are ever-fluctuating, running a co-op of 800 farmers requires not only business skills but also extensive interpersonal and effective communication skills. As Roberto put down the phone from a concerned farmer, he

A Panamanian coffee picker in Coope Dota

explained a dilemma that some of his farmers face. In principle, associates in the co-op agree to sell all their coffees through the co-op. In practice, things are not always so simple as some producers are pursued by other buyers who are willing to pay higher prices. The contracts with the co-op were agreed upon before the season began, fair at the time, and protected the farmers from a decline in prices during the year. However, in a year like 2011 where the commodity coffee price (known as the C-market) has nearly doubled in six months, there are buyers who will try any argument to coax the farmers to sell their recently picked crop. In this case, the buyer tried to convince the farmer that the co-op may not be liquid, a fabrication that Roberto timely refuted.

Perhaps the most inspiring aspect of the ingenuity I witnessed at Coope Dota is the productive utilization of every part of the coffee cherry. The skin and the pulp are collected and piled high in red mountains and then transported to a location overlooking the valley where the strong and pungent smell does not reach the town. Worms are inserted into the mix to eat the pulp and produce organic fertilizer that is then sold at very little cost back to the farmers. The mucilage is removed and used to produce ethanol on the premises. The husk (the harder covering of the bean) is removed and used for fueling the stoves that power the bean driers of the mill. Coope Dota has managed to completely eliminate the use of wood for heating their driers, yielding not only environmental benefits but also cost savings. As Roberto proudly notes, these processes have contributed to the co-op becoming 100% carbon-neutral, a goal they have been pursuing relentlessly for the last few years. Finally, the green bean that is left after husk removal is used, well ... to make coffee. ✑

EL SALVADOR: Excellent Coffees Emerging After the Civil War

THE ARRIVAL OF A TOP-OF-THE-LINE LA MARZOCCO GS3 ESPRESSO MACHINE on January 27, 2011 marked a momentous day at the offices of the J. Hill Mill in Santa Ana, El Salvador. This is where world-renowned Aida Batlle, a fifth-generation coffee farmer, oversees the sophisticated processing of some of the world's best specialty coffees that are grown on her three family-owned and one individually-owned farms. A few months earlier, Aida had made coffee history by becoming the first coffee producer to become a Level One certi-

A spectrum of coffee cherries. You want to pick only the ripest ones on the right.

Aida Batlle explaining some of the finer points of her coffee production.

fied barista by the Barista Guild of America. From this day on, she will be able to prepare killer cappuccinos for her co-workers while discussing the fine aspects of coffee processing with them. As luck would have it, a trio of visiting coffee enthusiasts who appreciated the magnitude of the new espresso machine's arrival was also as eager as she to inaugurate the machine: Raul Rodas from neighboring Guatemala who had won second place at the 2010 World Barista Championship, Roukiat Delrue, one of only a select few certified head judges for that competition, and a computer scientist turned coffee culturalist who was thrilled to reach Central America on his global coffee search route. After several hours of toiling around with the machine and even consulting with the instruction manual, the machine was set up and the first cappuccino emerged.

Aida's fascinating coffee career offers an intensely personal narrative of the turbulent history of El Salvador in the last few decades. No other country in the region has depended as deeply on what Salvadorans call "el grano de oro" (the "grain of gold"): coffee. By the 1970's, El Salvador had become the world's fourth largest exporter of coffee. As civil war broke out in the late 1970's, Aida's father received constant death threats. When one day the insurgent guerrillas kidnapped (and later released) a member of her family mistaking him for

[120]

The drying patios at J. Hill Mill

Aida's father, the Batlles decided the danger was too clear and present. While the family was on a trip accompanying Aida's older sister to the University of Miami in Florida, they decided to stay in the United States.

Aida was only six years old at the time and grew up in the U.S. with no connection to the family's coffee farming heritage. Throughout the civil war, her father kept traveling to El Salvador to operate the farms. In August 2002, Aida went back "home" to visit El Salvador. She realized the farms were run-down as a result of the war. Her father seemed tired and worried because of the depressed coffee prices at the time. Situated on the slopes of the Ilamatepec Volcano, the farms had excellent climate and altitude conditions to produce good coffee. However, they had been pushed to focus on quantity of production rather than quality. The poor shape of the farms in El Salvador after the war gave the country's coffee industry a bad reputation. After much soul-searching, Aida decided to take the plunge of leaving a comfortable job in Nashville Tennessee and moving back to El Salvador, a country she had not lived in for 24 years.

Upon returning to El Salvador, Aida faced a steep learning curve. Among the many challenges she faced were overcoming gender bias against a female "boss" like her, shifting the farm managers' focus from quantity of production to quality, and introducing experimental processing methods that were not previously used in El Salvador. Through hard work, resourcefulness, and sheer perseverance, Aida overcame each of these challenges. Even more remarkably, she had decided from the outset to gradually transform the family farms to being fully organic. This was tricky at a time when organic fertilizers were nowhere to be found in El Salvador. Knowing that yields from organic farms are much lower, this was also a risky business decision.

Soon after Aida's return, her aunt told her about the Cup of Excellence (CoE), the competition known as the "Oscars of Coffee." Not one to ever shy away from a challenge, Aida decided to enter samples from two of her farms in the competition. She instructed her pickers to pick the CoE samples by focusing only on blood reds and burgundies, the ripest of the cherries. She was understandably excited

Women sorting out the coffee beans before they are packed up.

when her Finca Los Alpes received the 16th spot in the competition. When her other farm, the Kilimanjaro, was announced as the first place winner, she was positively over the moon! Not only did she receive two awards, but she also became the first female farmer in fairly male-centric El Salvador to win this prestigious competition and the first woman anywhere in the world to win first place at a CoE competition!

The CoE win was a welcome boost to Aida's budding coffee farming career. First and foremost, it earned her respect on the farm. It was not easy for a woman who grew up in the United States to come to a coffee farm and start managing people who had been working there all their lives. She wanted her colleagues on the farm to respect her for the right reasons. Second, through the Cup of Excellence she came to know some of the coffee buyers she refers to as the "three originals": Solberg & Hansen from Norway, Counter Culture from Durham, North Carolina, and Ogawa Coffee from Japan. Over the years, the friendships that Aida developed with these buyers have helped her grow as a coffee producer. Today, her list of buyers includes some of the most highly respected roasters in the world. Pictures of perfectly ripe cherries from her Kilimanjaro and Mauritania farms are quick to be posted on Facebook and garner attention from coffee lovers worldwide. Aida has gone even further and designated a special "Aida's Grand Reserve" that is a blend of the peaberries from Finca Kilimanjaro, Finca Los Alpes, and Finca Mauritania, each processed differently.

Aida is a bubbly and self-professed workaholic whose emails seem to shoot from her blackberry phone directly into her bloodstream. As a fifth generation coffee grower, she now manages four farms that total 75 hectares and have an average annual production of 500 60kg bags of green coffee. Her great-great-grandfather Narciso Aviles, an army general and mayor of Santa Ana, the second largest city in El Salvador, is credited with bringing the Bourbon coffee varietal to the country. During the civil war, while other countries branched out by introducing better yielding and more disease-resistant varietals, El Salvador stayed the course with the Bourbon that is now one of its signature varietals. In 1958, El Salvador introduced the coffee world to the Pacamara varietal, which is a cross between Pacas (a mutation of Bourbon) and Maragogype. The Pacamara comes in two flavor profiles, one that is more floral and the other more herbal with a hint of green onion.

The coffee industry in El Salvador has gone through significant social change. It used to be dominated by 14 wealthy families. Land redistribution rules gave many of the indigenous families who worked the farms their own land. While redistribution was meant to level out the economic disparity in the country, it created a new set of problems because the families who received lands often lacked the skills to actually manage a farm.

Aida is a consummate experimentalist. One of her coffee cherry processing experiments led her onto a completely tangential career in tea production. One day as she entered the mill, she noticed that the pulp of the coffee cherry smelled like tamarind, roses and packed tobacco. She put a little bit in boiled water and the resulting mix yielded a surprisingly pleasant beverage. Even though it took a while to perfect the process, the blend is now known as Cascara Tea and is available through select coffee roasters. Interestingly, this kind of tea is not new. In fact, the Yemenites made a drink from the pulp of the coffee cherry (known as *qisher*) before they discovered the power of the bean inside. Qisher is still consumed in Yemen where coffee beans are used exclusively for export. However, they are clearly not processing the cherries as well as Aida, because they regularly add a collection of spices to make qisher palatable. The September 2010 Nordic Barista Cup even featured the debut of a limited run beer that was made from the cascara. Only time will tell whether Aida's fame from tea and other coffee cherry derivatives will overshadow her coffee processing prowess and the tremendous success of her highly prized coffees.

An hour's drive from the mill in the capital of El Salvador, San Salvador, Lily Pacas from the family that lent its name to the coffee varietal Pacas (a Bourbon mutation that first appeared in El Salvador in 1949) has been busy pushing El Salvador's coffee culture to new heights. Since founding Viva Espresso, Lily and her husband Federico Bolaños have dedicated countless resources to training baristas and encouraging them to compete. The top three baristas in the 2008 national championship of El Salvador were Lily, Federico and a member of their staff. Lily won the national title and went on to compete in the world championship. In fact, since El Salvador started conducting national barista championships, the winner has always been from Viva Espresso.

Two years later, Lily and Federico hired Alejandro Mendez, a college student looking for a job to make ends meet. They quickly realized that they have a young talent on their hands and put him through the famed Viva Espresso training. After winning the 2010 national barista championship, Alejandro made it to the semifinals during his debut appearance at the 2010 World Barista Championship in London. That appearance whet his appetite. The following year Alejandro delivered a mind-blowing performance in Bogotá, Columbia that should grace any textbook on coffee. Alejandro's signature drink consisted of four components that were all derived from the coffee tree. He began with a tea prepared from the leaf of the coffee tree, followed by a cascara made from the pulp, similar to Aida's creation. The third component demonstrated the sweetness of the mucilage surrounding the coffee bean by infusing beans covered with mucilage in hot water (the beans were harvested two months earlier and frozen to preserve the mucilage). The last component, espresso, was roasted especially for him by HasBean Coffee in Stafford, England. The brilliantly delivered performance made history. In front of a cheering crowd in Bogotá, Alejandro was declared World Barista Champion, the first from a coffee producing country. This milestone achievement earned El Salvador a distinguished role in the annals of competitive coffee. ✍

Alejandro Mendez with Lily Pacas and Federico Bolanos at the 2011 WBC awards ceremony.

COLOMBIA: Continuing the Juan Valdez Legacy

IN 2004 THE COFFEE FEDERATION OF COLOMBIA BEGAN ITS SEARCH for a successor to fill a highly coveted position in the country, the new face of Colombian coffee. They were not looking for a movie star or news celebrity, but rather, another affable Colombian farmer who can continue the legacy of Juan Valdez, the world famous icon. Standing by his coffee-carrying mule, the poncho-clad and sombrero-wearing Juan Valdez is by far the most well-known icon in coffee marketing history. He is also the most recognized Colombian, ahead of Colombian Nobel Laureate in literature Gabriel García Márquez and the infamous drug lord Pablo Escobar.

Portraying a humble Colombian coffee picker through the fictitious character of Juan Valdez was the brainchild of the National Federation of Coffee Growers of Colombia (FNC) and the New York ad agency Doyle Dane Bernbach. Launched in 1959, the wildly successful marketing campaign sought to connect a representative image from coffee's origin with the product sold in supermarkets. Its aura of romance and mystique persists today. In the United States alone, 85% of the population still associates the name Juan Valdez with fine Colombian coffee.

José F. Duval, a Cuban actor, portrayed Juan Valdez in both print advertisements and on television from 1959 until his death in 1969. The personification of Colombian coffee (most of which is grown at high altitudes and tended with painstaking care in the shade of banana and rubber trees) in the image of a humble farmer coming down from a quintessential hillside farm became an instant sensation. Within five months of the campaign, the number of people who identified Colombian coffees as being excellent rose by 300%. Sixty percent of consumers were willing to pay higher prices for Colombian coffee compared to only 4% before the campaign started. As the face of Juan Valdez appeared on coffee cans, cafés and major billboards in different parts of the world, Colombian coffee became synonymous with coffee excellence.

Farmer Carlos Sánchez from Fredonia succeeded Duval in 1970 as the second Juan Valdez. Sánchez's announced retirement necessitated a new search. The search committee of the FNC began with 380,000 registered farmers, an impressive candidate pool by any measure. Through several rounds of review, the committee narrowed the pool down to 406, 147, 30, and finally, to five candidates. The committee that included psychologists, publicists, and actors decided on Carlos Castañeda, a 39 year old farmer and father of three from the town of

Colombia's 2011 Barista Champion, Lina Zea, with Juan Valdez

Coffee farm in the Quindío region of Colombia

Andes, Antioquia, as the new Juan Valdez. Carlos was chosen not only on account of his uncanny resemblance to his predecessors but also his charming personality and charisma.

In a country where the vast majority of its 500,000 coffee farms are small and family-run operations, it is no coincidence that farmer Juan Valdez has become the embodiment of Colombian national pride that is inextricably linked to the excellence of its coffees. The arid mountains and the well-drained, rich volcanic soil of Colombia provide ideal conditions for growing

View of Buenavista
(on the left) from the
coffee farm at Finca
San Alberto in Colombia

exceptional coffees such as the Bourbon, Typica, Caturra, and Maragogype varietals. These highly flavorful, full-bodied, and perfectly balanced coffees are grown in two main regions: the central region around Medellin, Armenia and Manizales, known as MAM to aficionados, and the eastern region near Bogotá and Bucaramanga.

Even though coffee production now comprises less than 10% of Colombia's exports, it remains key to the national identity and reputation. For more than 60 years coffee had been the main export of Colombia (in 1976 this number was a whopping 84%). By 1930 Colombia had become the second biggest coffee producer in the world. It only slid to third position after Vietnam's meteoric rise in the late 20th century. The FNC, a private association that provides a multitude of benefits to its members, has been one of the most economically and politically powerful groups in the country. Other industries such as transportation and banking also evolved around coffee.

No one knows for sure when coffee first reached Colombia, though many historians believe it to be around the same time as the Jesuit priests first began arriving from Europe in the mid-16th century. The coffee that first arrived from Guyana through Venezuela was cultivated initially in the eastern part of the country. The leaders' attempt to encourage people to grow coffee met with resistance because a coffee tree usually takes four to five years to yield its first harvest. Thanks to a unique Colombian innovation that has been credited at least in folklore to a priest from Salazar de las Palmas named Francisco Romero, coffee cultivation not only came to pass but also spread to other parts of the country. Instead of the usual penance at confession, Father Francisco told his parishioners to plant three or four coffee trees to have their sins forgiven. The planting became the general practice after the Archbishop of Colombia ordered everyone to adopt this excellent idea. Coffee production expanded relatively quickly to central and western Colombia, where most of the country's production comes from today. The first record of commercial coffee production is from 1835 when Colombia exported 2,560 bags. Thanks to its unusual practice of proliferating coffee, today Colombia produces about 10 million bags of coffee annually. ✎

BRAZIL: Coffee Superpower

The Jequitiba tree, estimated to be over 1500 years old, is the symbol of the Sertaozinho Farm.

AS THE WORLD'S LEADING COFFEE PRODUCER, BRAZIL is responsible for 30% of the international coffee supply today, more than the next six major producing countries combined. After doubling its internal coffee consumption in the last 15 years, Brazil ranks second only to the United States in total coffee consumption. As may be expected, one of the characteristics of Brazilian coffee culture is the deep connection between production and consumption.

In 2002, Georgia Franco de Souza opened Lucca Cafés Especials, the first specialty Brazilian coffee shop in Curitiba, Paraná. Though she spent the first few years of her childhood on her grandfather's coffee farm and most summers helping out with the harvest, it took her a long time to realize her true coffee calling. Georgia had worked as a database administrator at a local university for years. However, after she spent a summer at a culinary school in France, she had an epiphany about culinary professionals: no matter how hard they worked, they were constantly smiling. She phoned her husband and told him: "*I also want to smile every day*" and promptly quit her database job. When she had to choose a branch of the culinary profession to smile at, coffee was the natural choice.

Georgia was also a personal witness to the most devastating event in Brazil's coffee industry, the Black Frost of 1975 that destroyed over one and a half billion trees. Though Brazilian farmers had known droughts and frosts, none had ever matched the scale and extent of damage that hit on July 17, 1975. When viewed from above, the farms looked black because the leaves had burned as the water that was trapped in them thawed. The Black Frost convinced many of the farmers in Paraná, until then the main coffee producing region of Brazil, to leave the area or start growing more sturdy crops such as corn and wheat. Many farmers moved from Paraná northward to Minas Gerais where they converted cattle farms into coffee plantations. On the international scene, world coffee prices doubled in the subsequent months in anticipation of low supply resulting from the Brazilian natural disaster. Georgia's grandfather Enzo Bonetto, who emigrated from Italy in 1929, died from a heart attack due to stress related to the Black Frost that completely destroyed his farm and ruined his livelihood.

To fully appreciate the impact of the Black Frost on Brazil, one needs to understand how coffee is inextricably entwined with the country's history and politics. Bringing coffee to Brazil required suave Brazilian finesse. The Brazilians were desperate to get their hands on coffee in the early 18th century. However, the beans were carefully guarded by the French who had brought them to the New World. The opening in the tight defense of the French came in 1727 when a dispute erupted between Dutch Guyana and French Guyana to the north. The King of Portugal dispatched Francisco de Mello Palheta to French Guyana to mediate between the two governors. While he successfully provided his mediation services, Palheta also managed to gain the affection of the French governor's wife. In return for his amorous services, the wife hid a few coffee seeds in a plant that she presented to him at a party held in his honor, thereby birthing the coffee industry of Brazil.

Despite Palheta's heroic deeds, it took about 40 years before coffee became a significant component of Brazil's agriculture. While the coffee industry drew a new wave of immigrants from Europe to plant new farms, the real work was done by a steady stream of slaves imported from Africa. The number of the slaves dwarfed those who went to North America. Over the span of 200 years, three million slaves were brought in to work on Brazil's coffee plantations, and five million others were brought to the sugarcane plantations. In comparison, the number of slaves in North America totaled about half a million. Brazil did not officially abolish slavery until 1888.

In the late 19th century, coffee accounted for over 60% of Brazil's exports and Brazil was responsible for 70% of the world's coffee supply. Given the frequent fluctuations in global coffee prices, it comes as no surprise that Brazil's politics and economic stability were closely linked to coffee prices. As coffee prices swung, so did political fortunes in Brazil. The coffee magnates were not shy to exert their influence. In 1889, they backed a military coup that drove out the emperor. Swings in coffee prices also played a significant role in Getúlio Vargas' rise to power to become Brazil's dictator in 1930 and in his suicide on August 24, 1954.

Even as the world's largest producer of coffee, Brazil did not garner respect on the international coffee scene in the early days. All coffee exports out of Brazil had been very tightly controlled by the government. Essentially, all coffees, no matter where they were grown or how they were processed, were deposited into one of four big bins of differing quality grades. This less than dazzling array of choices did not exactly inspire coffee buyers to take a deeper look into Brazil's coffees, nor did it give much incentive to farmers to distinguish themselves in any way. To make things worse, Brazil's coffees became generically known as Santos Coffees, named after the port from which they were exported, paying no tribute to the originating farms.

The seeds of Brazil's modern coffee industry as we know it today were sown in the 1980's. After Brazil emerged from military dictatorship, restrictions on exports were removed. Growers were able to directly export their own crops without going through the communal

A schoolhouse for workers' children at Fazenda Sertãozinho

bins. As it became possible for a farm to distinguish itself, the focus turned to improving quality and enhancing awareness of the range of Brazilian coffees. Concomitant with changes in labor laws which required farm owners to pay significant social benefits, larger farms began building housing units, schools for the workers' children, and community centers.

Leaders of the coffee industry founded the Brazilian Specialty Coffee Association in 1991. One of the key contributions of the association was developing strict quality control processes and ensuring transparency of the origins of the coffee. Farmers send samples of their coffee to get cupped and graded before they become eligible to bear the stamp of the association. When the bags of coffee are shipped, they each include an identification number that enables coffee buyers to track the origin and details about its production through the association's web site.

In the late 1990's, the quest to improve the image of Brazilian coffees inspired the Cup of Excellence, a competition among coffee growers that became known as the "Oscars of Coffee." Samples submitted to this competition are rigorously reviewed by a national jury followed by an international one. The coffees that pass muster end up being auctioned on the Internet and command significantly higher prices than on the normal specialty market. The competition has since been adopted by eight other coffee producing nations.

Coffee is grown in many areas of Brazil, with the largest producers located in Minas Gerais, Espiritu Santo, São Paulo, Paraná, and Bahia. Unlike its neighbors, almost all Brazilian coffees are grown at moderate elevations, ranging from 2,800 to 3,500 feet. As a result, Brazilian coffees are not known for featuring classic acidity like coffees from

Georgia Franco handing the 4th place trophy at the 2011 World Taster's Championship to her daughter Carolina in Maastricht, Netherlands.

Kenya, Ethiopia, Colombia or El Salvador. Instead, they are prized for their sweetness and softer and rounder mouth feel, making them more approachable by a broader client base and good choices for roasters to use as the basis for their espresso blends.

Unfortunately, the quality of the coffees available to the masses in Brazil is generally very poor compared to the specialty coffees that are earmarked for export and prized on the international market. The traditional and ubiquitous Brazilian coffee drink, the *cafézinho*, is designed to boldly mask the low quality of the coffee. The cafézinho is prepared by first mixing sugar with water, then bringing the mixture to a boil, and finally

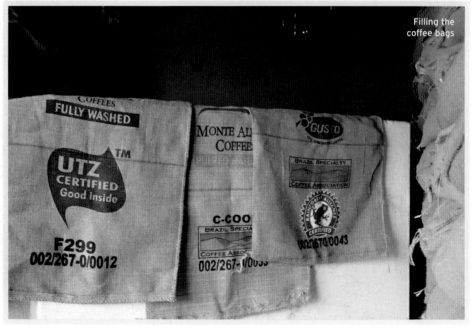

Filling the coffee bags

stirring in the coffee grounds. The coffee is poured into the cup through a cloth filter that can be found in many stores in Brazil. If you can still taste the coffee after these steps, you are free to put in as much milk as your heart desires.

Thankfully, change is under way. The specialty café scene in Brazil is definitely on the rise. Georgia, who now owns two cafés in Curitiba, laments that her greatest challenge is educating her clientele who had been accustomed to having only two coffee options: sweet or black. Georgia revels in educating the younger generation, starting as close to home as possible. Her own daughter Carolina started cupping coffee at the age of 12. When she was barely tall enough to reach the cups on top of the espresso machine, Carolina became the youngest person to ever compete in a barista competition. At the age of 19, Carolina had already won the Brazilian Cupping Championship. She represented Brazil at the 2010 WBC in London and placed 11th among 40 competitors. A year later she placed fourth in the World Cup Tasters Championship in Maastricht, Netherlands.

In São Paulo, Marco Suplicy's story also juxtaposes farmer and barista. The grandson of a coffee exporter of French descent, Marco spent many years in the financial industry as a stockbroker. Even though his wife's family has owned a farm for over 150 years and he was officially the manager of the farm, running a coffee farm full-time was just not his "cup of tea." With his boundless energy, Marco decided to open specialty cafés to showcase different Brazilian coffees. Beginning with a location in the hottest part of São Paulo, Marco has been steadily expanding his chain and now owns six cafés in the city and one in Brasilia. São Paulo, which prides itself on being the "biggest Italian city outside of Italy," has given Marco's cafés the thumbs up. Local food critics have showered praises thanking him for bringing "real" Italian espresso to the city.

Café Suplicy, São Paulo

In keeping with his mission to promote Brazilian coffee culture, Marco has become a master at fostering a vibrant barista culture. Among other activities, his cafés host monthly speed latte art contests known as "latte throwdowns." Baristas from around town come to compete, each contributing $10 to a central pot. At the end of the evening, the winner walks away with the entire lot, making a pretty profitable evening.

To get started with his café chain, Marco had sought external consultation to design his café and related workflow. He ended up engaging Sherri Johns, an American café expert. Sherri's services included designing different aspects such as layout and seating, and training the staff. His quip summarizes the irony of coffee consumption in Brazil: "*We had to get an American to show Brazilians how to drink coffee.*" ✎

ASIA & THE PACIFIC RIM

Ever since the Sufi pilgrim Baba Budan returned from Yemen to India in 1600 with seven live coffee seeds in his pouch, Southeast Asia and the Pacific Rim have played a notable part in the world's coffee production. Thanks to the Dutch who ran the most powerful maritime operation in the 17th century and managed to transport coffee from Yemen to Java and beyond, names such as Java and Sumatra have become synonymous with coffee. By the end of the 17th century, coffee production from the East Indies had caught up with those of Yemen and Ethiopia and later surpassed them. Fast forward to the end of the 20th century. Recovering from its war and with financial assistance from international organizations, Vietnam emerged as and remains the second largest coffee grower in the world albeit of the less respected Robusta species. China is planning to triple its coffee production in the coming years.

This section explores the consumption side of coffee in the Pacific Rim, which offers some of the most surprising discoveries of my tour of world coffee. In Australia, Melbourne in particular, we experience one of the most invigorating café cultures in the world where there is an amazing concentration of world-class cafés within walking distance from each other (some with names such as Baba Budan and Seven Seeds). In Japan, we witness a very sophisticated coffee culture with refined sense of aesthetics where the clientele is willing to pay top dollars for the world's most prized beans. As a result, Japanese coffee importers are busy scouring coffee farms around the world in search of the best lots. In South Korea, we discover an extremely entrepreneurial coffee culture. In sections of Seoul where there may be three different cafés in one building, Korean entrepreneurship has invented cleverly effective ways of product and service differentiation. In China, we stumble upon a mixture of nostalgic coffee culture among the Western-educated and an emerging coffee culture where the young now routinely choose cafés over tea houses as preferred venues for social gatherings. All of this is just the tip of the iceberg for a country with an incredible potential for explosive growth in coffee appreciation and consumption.

Kanon Coffee, 798 Art
District, Beijing

AUSTRALIA: A Rich Coffee Culture Down Under

Seven Seeds Café

AUSTRALIA IS NOT STEEPED in the history of Europe's grand literary cafés. Furthermore, when the British fleet arrived in Sydney Harbor on January 26, 1788, they did not offer cups of java to the aborigines. Yet Australia enjoys one of the most sophisticated coffee cultures in the world. I was first exposed to this culture while touring London's coffee scene, where the majority of the new coffee shops are founded by Antipodeans (a U.K. term of endearment for Aussies and Kiwis). My leaving-no-stones-unturned research attitude prompted me to seize on the first opportunity I had to dive Down Under.

I'm often asked to reflect on my extensive coffee-related travel and identify my favorite places. If I had the luxury to spend my life wandering from one great café to another, I would most certainly settle in Melbourne, Australia. Nowhere else have I seen so many terrific cafés in such close proximity and wanted to spend hours in each. As a consequence, my visit to Melbourne turned out to be the most caffeinated day of my life. Fortunately, I was armed with excellent café-hopping tips from Emily Oak, with whom I became acquainted through an article in *Barista Magazine*. Emily is the training and development director for Australian Independent Roasters in Sydney. She serves on the board of directors of the World Barista Championship, the organization that oversees the annual competitions. She also represented Australia at the second WBC in 2001. Most importantly, Emily *knows* coffee in Australia. She graciously furnished all the information I needed before, during, and after my visit Down Under.

After a 15-hour flight from San Francisco, I hit the ground running in Melbourne by starting my tour at the Seven Seeds Café. It is difficult not to have high expectations from a café whose web site boasts: *"Our aim is simple. To provide first class coffee. We are relentless."* And the place did not disappoint. The quality of the coffee, the preparation, and the skill of the baristas were all world-class. This is the first place where I caught a glimpse of the creative food menus available in many Australian cafés. Moreover, the ambiance was beautiful. The coffee-themed wall decor spotlighted drawings of coffee bushes, coffee equipment, and a map of coffee's spread around the world. Even the placement of utensils and menus inside empty boxes of bullets seemed charming. Notwithstanding its intricate decor, the café had a down-to-earth and comfortable feel. I sat at one of the community tables and struck up conversation with a local couple. From their vast knowledge I immediately realized how deep-rooted coffee culture is in this city. As my new buddy put it, *"In Melbourne, when we want to go out for a drink, we go to a café."*

Seven Seeds is the creation of Bridget Amor and Mark Dundon, serial entrepreneurs and trendsetters on the Melbourne coffee scene. Their latest café is named De Clieu, after the French army captain whose legendary trip across the Atlantic Ocean, while heroically guarding a coffee plant, is credited with bringing coffee to South and Central America. Mark had founded and later sold St. Ali Café. He also owns Brother Baba Budan, named after the Sufi who had secretly smuggled seven coffee seeds from the port of Mocha in Yemen to India in the 17th century, thereby considerably extending the reach of coffee around the world. The café's trademark is the chairs hanging from its ceiling. In fact, that ceiling furnishing has been copied in cafés from New Zealand to Seoul.

Another typical Melbourne experience awaited me at the Auction Rooms, a few blocks away from Seven Seeds. Owner Andrew Kelly hosted me graciously. He and Jason Scheltus, the Director of Coffee at Market Lane Coffee, another one of Melbourne's fine cafés, gave me the lowdown on the coffee scene in town. Merely two hours after landing in Melbourne, I already felt well-connected in this close-knit coffee community.

My next stop was a highly recommended educational experience (note to visitors: please avoid my mistake of arriving there already caffeinated). Situated at the entrance to the David Jones Department Store in downtown, the Sensory Lab is the place to learn about the newest and most trendy brewing technologies. While serving the casual customer who needs a pre-shopping boost, the lab really caters to serious coffee geeks. You begin by filling out a questionnaire specifying which coffee bean you want with each of four brews: an espresso-based piccolo (small latte), a hand-dripped cup, a siphon brew, and the cold brew. It is recommended to try the same bean for each of the brews so you can discern the differences resulting from the brewing techniques (though of course you are welcome to pick whichever bean suits your fancy). I chose the Geisha Coffee for my siphon brew (this coffee is the subject of an entire book by Michaele Weissmann, where it became known as "God in a Cup"), and a blend of Ethiopian Yirgacheffe and Kenya Gaikundo for the others. I sat there for a long while, pondering the differences among the coffee preparations and wondering when my head would explode from all the caffeine I had consumed in the last three hours. When I realized that my body would survive the experience, I set out to investigate the older Melbourne cafés which are fortunately known more for their food and desserts than the latest and greatest in coffee.

High standards for coffee in Melbourne took root in the 1950s when the city enjoyed a large wave of migration from Italy and other parts

Café Baba Budan, famous in part for its hanging chairs. Apparently there was nowhere else to put them.

A table preparation at the Sensory Lab in Melbourne.

of Europe. Those immigrants came with their espresso machines. They began spreading coffee culture around the city and ultimately throughout Australia. Pellegrini's Espresso, a local institution since 1954, provides a flavor of those early days. Well-preserved with its nostalgic decor, the centerpiece consists of one long bar along which patrons can sit and drink coffee (or, in my over-caffeinated state, a watermelon-flavored granita) or have a quick Italian meal (I know, a contradiction in terms). If you need dessert, or 100 of them to choose from, head to Café Brunetti on the famous Lygon Street where the scrumptious pastry selection can keep you hostage for hours.

I could not leave Melbourne without visiting Nolan Hirte, the local Master Tinkerer. After a brisk early morning walk through Melbourne's flawed conception of summer in January, I was the first customer at Proud Mary, a new café founded by Nolan and his wife. Nolan, a former Western Australia Barista Champion and founder of Liar Liar, another Melbourne coffee establishment, has been applying his passion for building and modifying things to coffee machines. During a visit to Canada, Nolan was inspired by an espresso machine with five(!) group heads. Not to one-up his inspiration, Nolan proceeded to assemble a machine with six group heads from two three-head Synesso machines (keep in mind that most cafés do just fine with two or three heads). He did not stop there. He also equipped the Proud Mary with six coffee grinders that have been modified to exceed the wildest expectations of grinding experts. The consummate result of all this tinkering is that every type of bean Nolan grinds has its own group head, ultimately producing drinks of purer taste.

Sydney also boasts a dynamic coffee culture, though the best cafés are not as closely situated as in Melbourne. My visit to Sydney could not have started any better: Em-

The code at The Source.

ily, my hitherto virtual guide, whisked me from the airport in a car smelling of the fresh coffee beans she had just delivered to a customer. We started at Coffee Alchemy, the brainchild of Hazel de Los Reyes whose passion for coffee began with her grandmother's coffee trees back in the Philippines and has been truly relentless ever since. Hazel has amassed an impressive number of titles, including the 2005 Australia Barista Champion and 2007 Australian Cupping Champion. After enjoying a wonderful El Salvadorian coffee, I learned my first Australian expression of the day. Emily asked whether I would like to take a "*sticky beak.*" When my reserved agreement failed to conceal my utter confusion at her proposal, she explained that it means taking a look in the back of the café.

Nolan Hirte operating his unique self-assembled 6-group head espresso machine at his café, Proud Mary, in Melbourne, Australia.

I was sure glad for the clarification. It was fascinating to see Hazel operate a spanking new roaster with her awesome collection of trophies and medals in the backdrop.

We then headed to The Source Espresso Bar where I was let in on the secret "code." At most coffee establishments, baristas mark on the cups the exact drink that the customers request. At The Source, there is a much more sophisticated coding system. The drinks are encoded by the size of the saucer and the position and orientation of the spoon on the saucer. For example, small saucer with a spoon on top is a macchiato. If you move the spoon to the right, it would signify a picollo latte. Put the same spoon on a larger saucer, and you get either a cappuccino or a latte. If the spoon moves to the middle, a hot chocolate; but if it moves to the left, a mocha. Rumor has it that there is also a special code to mark an especially attractive customer, but no one I spoke with would confirm or deny that allegation.

Our last stop was at Mecca Espresso in downtown Sydney. This café caters to the fast-paced lifestyle of the office crowd. Mostly from the financial industry (think Wall Street, but with an Australian accent), they demand their coffee quickly but without quality compromises. At Mecca Espresso, customers are guaranteed a good morning jolt through excellent coffee and the baristas' jolly maneuvers around the machines. When you visit, try to have an up close and personal look at Sebastian Butler-White. The coffee-themed tattoo on his arm will convince you that you are getting coffee from extremely dedicated staff.

In sum, Australians do take their coffee seriously. Their signature drink is the flat white, which is most similar to the American conception of the latte, though typically smaller. Its sibling, the long black, is most similar to an americano (espresso with added hot water). Australians have been a true force on the international coffee scene, often making it to the finals at the WBC and even winning when Paul Bassett competed in 2003. In 2010, Australia was recognized as Best Nation for its overall achievements in the various world championships of the year. ✎

Stomp Espresso,
Brisbane

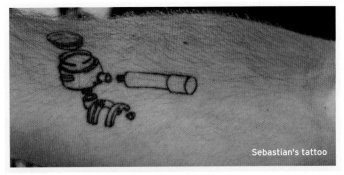

Sebastian's tattoo

2010 Australian
barista team

JAPAN: Relentless Pursuit of Quality Coffee

"YES, I'M GOING TO JAPAN FOR THE COFFEE." I had to assert repeatedly to friends who were fixated on the pleasures of fresh sashimi accompanied by sake and delicate Japanese tea. Much to the surprise of many, Japan is the third largest importer of coffee in the world. Because Japanese consumers are willing to pay more for a better cup of coffee, Japan imports very high quality beans from the world's most exceptional growers. In particular, it imports more Cup of Excellence winning coffees than any other country.

Tokyo is probably the city in which you are least likely to taste a bad cup of coffee. If you know where to go, the coffee will be superb. Even though innovations in espresso preparation are not immediately associated with Japan, the Japanese have not only endowed the world with an industry of canned coffee beverages, but also some of the most sophisticated coffee brewing machines available today. The trendy Blue Bottle Café in San Francisco proudly exhibits a Japanese drip coffee machine. Cafés in Melbourne sell Japanese siphon brewers, the latest in coffee brewing technology.

Japanese cafés, known as *kissaten*, started appearing shortly after the Dutch brought coffee to its shores around 1877, initially in Tokyo and then throughout the country. As in Europe, cafés became places for people to socialize and play games. To distinguish themselves from the competition, cafés often specialized in a particular kind of music or activity.

Following the footsteps of John Rain, who starred in the award-winning thrillers of Barry Eisler as a Japanese-American hired assassin, is a terrific way to tour of some of the treasures among Tokyo's coffeehouses. Rain was always in the crosshairs of one or more organizations: a lethal renegade Japanese political faction, the CIA, or some *femme fatale* who typically ended up in his bed. Constantly looking over his shoulders and taking a circuitous route everywhere he went, Rain frequented several cafés in Tokyo for his meetings.

Hatou Café near the Shibuya train station provides a wonderful vista into Japanese coffee culture at its best. The windowless L-shaped café is marked by a long counter where patrons may sit and view the barista hand-brewing each cup of coffee. The wall behind the bar is lined with shelves displaying dainty porcelain cups and saucers of all shapes and designs. You can choose the country of origin you want your coffee to be brewed from and expect each cup to be prepared with utmost care and attention. To quote Eisler as he watched the barman slowly pouring water from the pot onto the filter in round motions, "*He looked like he was painting or conducting a miniature orchestra.*" Slow and circular motion ensures the even flow of water through the coffee. An Italian colleague who accompanied me to the café reacted to the orchestral tempo of coffee preparation: "*An Italian barista would be hospitalized in a mental institution by now!*" East/West cultural contrasts aside, the coffee was definitely worth the wait. We were tickled pink to discover that the Japanese couple at the adjacent table was also following the footsteps of John Rain.

Another distinctively Japanese experience awaits at Tsuta coffeehouse where to the backdrop of classical music, the owner Koyama-san has been personally brewing each cup for over 20 years. With a few chairs along the bar and two tables next to a big window looking into an indoor garden, Tsuta is a very cozy place. In fact, it was John Rain's top choice for a first date. Koyama-san was brewing coffee and chatting with

The barista at Hatou Café patiently hand pours a coffee.

his customers on a Saturday night when I entered way past the official closing hours. I felt like I was crashing a private six-person party. Foolishly imagining that I could blend in inconspicuously, I sat at the bar quietly and ordered my coffee. Within minutes, curiosity and Japanese hospitality overtook language barriers and everyone in the café wanted to know everything about me.

Tokyo excels at catering to foreigners. In his more relaxed moments, Rain had frequented cafés where he did not have to hide in the back. A short walk from the Takadanobaba Station on the Yamanote Line is Ben's Café. Sitting on a side street and meandering into a small courtyard, it could have been transplanted from any European or American city. Patrons can order espresso drinks and their favorite western-style sandwich, or attend any of the concerts the café advertises on its Facebook page. At Las Chicas, tucked away on a quiet street corner in the Shibuya area, customers are greeted by foreign staff (mostly Brazilian when I visited) before settling into the pleasurable enjoyment of a coffee or a meal.

For a taste of the specialty coffee scene in Tokyo, try Bar Del-Sol at Roppongi, home of one of the most famous Japanese baristas, Chihiro Yokoyama. In the Shinjuku area, visit Paul Bassett Café, a joint venture between the 2003 World Barista Champion from Australia and the 1997 World Patissier Champion Hironobu Tsujiguchi. Bassett's menu allows the customers to choose their preferred latte art patterns.

When in the mood for nostalgia, visit the Meikyoku Kissa Lion café in Tokyo's Shibuya district. The Lion has not changed at all since its founding in 1926. The café can best be described as a cross between a train car and a theater. As in a train, the chairs are arranged to face mostly towards the front, with the occasional backward facing seats to allow for four-way conversation. The centerpiece at the front of the theater is a huge sound system that is flanked by shelves containing thousands of LP records and emanating classical music. Most of the clientele are either individuals coming to take a coffee break or spend some time with course work. Smoking is only allowed on the second floor, which is also arranged to enable patrons to face the sound system. The café was dark and the menu simple. Even though photos were not allowed despite multiple requests, the coffee (whose preparation was hidden from view) was adequate.

The first Starbucks store outside the U.S. opened in Tokyo in 1996 to great fanfare. People had lined up for hours in anticipation of the opening. As the ribbon was cut, the first customer darted into the store and uttered his drink order with the same pride of winning an Olympic gold medal.

A plastic food sample of latte art at Paul Bassett Café in Shinjuku.

Koyama-san, the proprietor of Tsuta pouring coffee as he chats with his clientele.

The concept of cookie-cutter cafés where you can grab a coffee and a bite to eat on-the-go was invented in Japan as early as 1971 by Hiromichi Toriba. Toriba was inspired to open a coffee business while studying coffee in São Paolo, Brazil. During a trip to Paris a few years later, he noticed that on their way to work many people drank coffee and munched on croissants. Convinced that the Japanese workforce would need a similar coffee ritual, Toriba opened the Doutor chain that rode the wave of Japan's economic boom and grew rapidly. Interestingly, Starbucks bolstered Doutor's revenues that were starting to flatten around that time. Doutor responded to Starbucks' entry by opening a sister chain, Excelsior Caffe. The new chain attracted a younger and mostly female clientele with its better lighting and separate smoking areas. For those who don't even have the time to order a coffee in the morning (or the inclination to speak that early in the day), Japanese cities are littered with coffee vending machines that either grind and brew the coffee for you on the spot or stand ready to spew out myriad types of canned coffee products.

Kentaro Maruyama, owner of Maruyama Coffee Company, best personifies Japan's esteemed role in today's specialty coffee crowd. Kentaro is considered by many to be the most discerning coffee taster in the world and is certainly one of the most respected and liked figures in the industry. Kentaro began his coffee business as a small roaster in his hometown of Karuizawa, about 200km northwest of Tokyo. Karuizawa is known in Japan as a high-class summer resort for the royal family and politicians. In collaboration with other small roasters in Japan, Kentaro created a "*mikataju*" (loosely "free school for [coffee] supporters"). As the best English speaker of the group, his translations of portions of the Specialty Coffee Association of America's (SCAA) web site for his pals have consistently aroused great excitement.

To further their coffee expertise, Kentaro volunteered to be a scout at the SCAA's Annual Conference in 2000. Since his mikataju buddies would not let him go alone, they set out on the mission together. That trip instilled in them a strong desire to become more immersed in the specialty coffee industry. As small-scale roasters, they decided to focus their energies on the Cup of Excellence competitions where growers compete on the quality of their crop and winners have the opportunity to sell their lots in an Internet auction. These competitions always offer an intimate setting to get to know other coffee buyers from around the world and to learn about coffees from different regions. Moreover, the sizes of the lots being sold at the auctions were closer to what the mikataju could afford. They were elated when they won a lot at the 2001 CoE competition in Guatemala, the first such competition they had ever attended. Soon after securing their winning bid, Kentaro was invited to serve as a judge in the competition. He has since been a staple at these competitions, spending much of his time on the road.

In 2002, Kentaro's team shocked the industry by bidding $12.85 per pound for the No.1 lot "Agua Limpa II" from Brazil. *"I couldn't tolerate that this superb coffee go to somebody else,"* he explained. Over the years, Japanese companies have been able to buy a large portion of the winning CoE coffees because unlike some of their American counterparts, the Japanese clientele is willing to pay much higher prices for outstanding products. Backed by this cultural asset, Kentaro has been able to win the first place lots in several other com-

Maruyama Coffee in Komoro

Mie Nakahara competing at the WBC in London, June 2010

Miki Suzuki competes at the 2011 WBC in Colombia. On the right, the card Miki presented the judges explaining the combination of flavors they will experience in her signature drink.

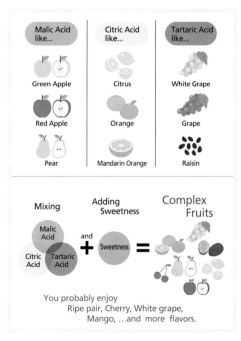

petitions, solidifying the reputation of Karuizawa as "*the place to go taste Maruyama Coffee.*"

A trip to Japan would not be complete without visiting Maruyama Coffee. I made the two-hour train trek out of Tokyo to Komoro, a city near Karuizawa where one of the newest Maruyama coffee shops had just opened. Here I was in for a double treat. In addition to tasting delicious Maruyama coffee, I was hosted by Mie Nakahara, the reigning (2009) Barista Champion of Japan. Coming from Tokyo where every square inch is packed to the gills, I was surprised to see an incredibly spacious café with a tall vaulted ceiling and floor-to-ceiling windows. It all made sense once Mie explained that the space had been converted from a car dealership.

After pulling me a shot of a single-origin Bolivian espresso, Mie cheerfully recounted her journey into coffee. She became fascinated with coffee when she worked in a café in Florence. She lamented the fact that the Italians never trusted her at the bar—a petite Japanese woman somehow just did not fit the preferred image of an Italian barista. Upon reflection, she playfully admitted that she couldn't really blame the Italians because "*I would never trust sushi made by an Italian.*"

Mie is a great testament to the nurturing side of Kentaro Maruyama the mentor. After returning from Italy, she started working at Maruyama Coffee where she and her colleagues have enjoyed the best training possible. Highlights of Maruyama's rigorous and spare-no-expense training have included special sessions with Fritz Storm, the 2002 World Barista Champion from Denmark, and trips to origin such as Costa Rica and Guatemala. After winning second place in the Japanese Barista Championship in 2008, the pressure was on in 2009 because none of the Maruyama baristas had ever won the Japanese title. Mie was one of six competitors that Maruyama Coffee sent to the 160-participant event. All six made it to the semifinals, but only Mie made it to the final round. She captured the title with a signature drink that featured honey made from the coffee flower and very large grapes, and by doing what very few Japanese dare to do—presenting in English. The following year, Miki Suzuki, another Kentaro protégé, stood proud at the 2011 WBC finals in Bogotá, Colombia where she placed fifth. ✍

THE REPUBLIC OF KOREA: Nation on a Café Craze

KOREANS LIKE TO TAKE THINGS TO EXTREMES. THEIR PASSION FOR COFFEE IS NO EXCEPTION. As of 2009, there were 200 'coffee academies' in Seoul and about the same number in Korea's second largest city Busan. In the first six months of 2009 alone, these academies certified 5,000 baristas! Whether you actually want to be a barista is completely irrelevant. In Seoul today, the goal is to have a barista certificate. Even housewives try to obtain a barista certificate, believing it will improve their homemaking skills. A coffee academy is typically the size of a studio apartment that is equipped with the full gamut of coffee paraphernalia, including a roasting machine, high-end espresso machine, grinders and all the latest hand-dripping equipment. These coffee academies teach their students about all aspects of coffee, from roasting and preparation to cupping.

The exact source of this craze is difficult to pin down. The American military introduced coffee to Korea during the Korean War in the early 1950s. Because only instant coffee was offered, it took a while for Koreans to shake the instant habit. Yunson Lee, now a Vice President at Terarosa Coffee, recalls that when she started selling fresh beans to Korean clients, they used to come back and complain that the coffee did not dissolve in their cups as they expected. Starbucks' arrival in 1999 heralded the flourishing of Korea's coffee culture. However, most Koreans did not hear of specialty coffee or learn of the barista profession until the summer 2007 airing of a TV series called *Coffee Prince*. The star of the drama was the scion of an affluent family who was trying to prove to his grandmother that he could do good by running a coffee shop. At the same time, he found himself falling in love with one of his male baristas and troubled by this newly discovered tendency. The barista turned out to be a female who pretended to be male to secure the male-only job. Love and questions about sexuality aside, the drama exposed Koreans to the glory of being a barista.

A café in Seoul with jars of beans from different origins and plenty of pour-over equipment.

A typical "coffee academy" in Seoul. Below, a sample of coffee drinks at a Seoul subway stop.

I must confess that South Korea was not on my radar screen at the outset of this book project when I mapped out my trips. However, I became intrigued when the Korean representative Lee JongHoon made it to the finals round and came in fifth place at the 2009 World Barista Championship. A month later when I needed to spend a day in Seoul on a trip around the world, I decided to pay JongHoon a visit.

JongHoon, or Barista Hoon as he is better known, is a very humble chap who had already distinguished himself as a barista champion by the age of 24. He began working as a barista during high school. At the age of 20, he won the 2004 inaugural Korean Barista Championship. He went on to represent Korea in the WBC in Trieste, Italy that year and finished 24th. In 2008 he won second place in the "Coffee World in Good Spirits" competition in Copenhagen.

JongHoon made history in 2009 as he regained the Korean national barista title and represented Korea at the WBC in Atlanta. He had become a much more refined and confident competitor on the world stage this time, and with much better English skills to boot. As he took the floor for his performance at the finals, fellow competitors described him as "beyond excited." He finished in 5th place, the first time a Korean had landed in the top ten! Upon returning to Korea, he received ample media attention and appeared on several national TV shows.

JongHoon's signature drink at the WBC was very revealing of his personality. He explained to the judges that he chose ingredients from coffee-growing countries in order to help the children of those countries. He named the drink "Republic of Coffee Zone" after his company. It included ground Venezuelan cacao, Madagascar vanilla bean, star anise from Jamaica, organic cane sugar from Colombia, and coffee beans from Ethiopia.

When JongHoon came to pick me up at 10am to start a private tour of Seoul's cafés, I had just arrived on a red-eye flight from Cambodia where my main coffee experience was an hour long body rub of coffee grounds mixed in massage oil that left me relaxed and smelling like a tall cappuccino for a full 24 hours. I was more than ready for a different form of caffeine intake.

After a brief stop at the subway station to view the bewildering array of canned coffee beverages available, we started our 12-hour journey near Ehwa Women's University. This area is known as the epicenter of coffee culture in Seoul because there are multiple cafés on each block and some buildings boast more than one.

In a competitive environment like this, Korean entrepreneurship kicks in big time as each café tries its best to distinguish itself. For example, when we walked into the Dog Café, 20(!) dogs welcomed us and kept us company while we checked out the coffee menu. Not a dog person? No worries. A few blocks down we found the Cat Café, which was admittedly a bit more sedate. The Kaldi Café (downstairs from the Kaldi Coffee Academy) had more of an old world feel. When we walked by the café that served as the set scene for *Coffee Prince*, I was warned that I would have to pay a royal premium for the pleasure of drinking there.

One of the fascinating aspects of Seoul coffee culture is how the rituals of tea drinking have been seamlessly applied to coffee. Several cafés displayed small containers that were each filled with coffee beans from a different region of the world. The barista will hand-drip a customized cup just for you after you choose from among the coffees, just as you would from an array of tea leaves.

The most unforgettable experience came when JongHoon took me to the Coffee Sum, a relatively new coffee establishment. The vision of the founding entrepreneurs was to combine multiple coffee experiences in one fantasy location. (In Korean, '*sum*' means island, making a play on words). The swanky café named "Coffee of Dream," the 'coffee factory' exhibiting the different stages of coffee production, and the zen garden were just warm-ups for the main event, the "coffee dark room." In preparation for entering the dark room, the guide requested that we store all our belongings in a locker, including our eyeglasses. The only thing we were allowed to take inside was a cane—that's really all we ended up needing in the

Coffee of Dream

The Dog Café

pitch dark. The guide explained that our objective was to deepen our coffee knowledge by learning about it through only our non-visual senses.

We made our way into a room, which felt eerily like walking through a forest on a very dark night. As we passed over a wobbly wooden bridge, we heard birds chirping and a water stream bubbling in the background. We had no idea how large the room was or how far we had walked or would walk. At our first stop, the guide verified that our entire group of six was intact and then asked us to bend down and search for the coffee bush amidst several

Lee JongHoon at his Coffee Lab.

bushes within our reach. After a short discussion about the results of the exercise, we continued walking (perhaps into a cave), and were asked to identify the single box of coffee beans from among several boxes that our hands were able to touch. At that stage, my cohorts and I were starting to feel more at ease in the darkness and jokes in Korean started to flow (a few of which were translated into English for my benefit). After twenty more minutes of walking around "in nature," we were led back into the café. Shockingly, we were still on the 13th floor of an office tower in the middle of a bustling city! Coffee Sum's owners kindly offered delicious coffee and cakes as we kicked back to ponder the rather unique experience. As in any entrepreneurially adventurous environment, not all ideas endure. I was sad to hear that the coffee dark room closed a few months after my visit, but glad to know that the café remains open.

At this point we needed a break from cafés. Barista Hoon and I hopped into a cab and headed to his "coffee lab." The cab took us to an apartment complex on the outskirts of Seoul where we walked up narrow stairs into a tiny flat. This is where JongHoon spends his time training the next generation of baristas, many of whom are older than he. Besides an impressive display of JongHoon's many awards, the lab is equipped with all the gear one would expect from a coffee lab: an espresso machine, a hefty roasting machine, and an amazing collection of espresso tampers. He teaches his students the art of roasting and brewing espresso, trains them to cup coffee and experience the subtle tastes, and, of course, to be a showman and create latte art.

After a very authentic Korean dinner, we topped off our day with a visit to one of JongHoon's most illustrious students, Yoo JungHyun. JungHyun is the 2008 Korean Barista Champion and one of the current head baristas at Café Themselves, a trendy café in the Insadong area. As in many other cafés in Seoul, the baristas recognized JongHoon and a crowd surrounded him immediately. I challenged his fan club to explain the meaning of "Café Themselves." Alas, with all their elaborate hand motions, they succeeded only at amusing themselves.

As we bid goodbye, I asked JongHoon about his plans for the future. He unhesitatingly indicated that he would like to "*get serious about coffee, study economics, and ultimately my own café.*" About a year later, JongHoon opened his own café, The Republic of Coffee.

CHINA: East Meets West for Coffee

CHINA, THE QUINTESSENTIAL TEA NATION! How are coffee lovers to cope when visiting or residing there?

Walk around the trendy 798 Art District of Beijing, and you will find no fewer than 25 cafés and only one teahouse. Stroll around Shanghai, and you can choose from 60 different chains or from a plethora of independently owned cafés serving coffee in this glitzy metropolis. Trek beyond the "first-tier" cities, and you are more likely to land back in the Republic of Tea. In cities like Shenyang (a city of "only" seven million people in northeastern China), you will at least have the option to settle for Starbucks.

Admittedly, coffee is not (yet!) for everyone in China. To put things in perspective, if the Chinese were to develop an addiction to the brew on a similar scale to that of the Americans, the world would have to double its production of coffee. Like many Western imports, coffee in China is consumed and enjoyed for the most part by the young and upwardly mobile, the intelligentsia, the Western educated, and the nouveau riche. Their desires to embrace and immerse in the chic, intellectual, romantic, or sometimes endearingly idiosyncratic ambiance attract them to cafés.

Sitting in a café or holding a Starbucks cup on the move is considered somewhat of a status symbol here. Starbucks came to China in 2000 when this tea stronghold was still virgin coffee territory, and became an instant hit. As part of its plan to become ubiquitous worldwide, Starbucks even opened a branch inside the Forbidden City, the residence of Chinese emperors for almost 500 years until the fall of the Qing Dynasty in 1912. The audacious intrusion touched a sensitive nerve and offended many Chinese. After seven years of mounting public pressure, that branch was forced to close. Despite such a highly publicized cultural clash with Chinese emotions, Starbucks continues to enjoy its first mover advantage and remains successful in China today. It currently operates around 70 branches in Beijing alone and serves as a frame of reference that propels the country's nascent specialty coffee industry.

Other chains are competing in the vast and highly segmented Chinese market by providing alternatives such as an Italian coffee experience (e.g. Costa Coffee whose offerings include tiramisu latte and hazelnut cappuccino, as well as an array of *dolci* and *panini*)

Thinker's Café in Beijing's Silicon Alley.

Bookworm café, Beijing

Coffee Tree Café, French Concession, Shanghai

or a taste of Taiwanese coffee culture (e.g. 85C Bakery Café). These chains are by no means courting customers by promoting the latest in single-origin espressos. To many Chinese consumers, paying the equivalent of $3 for a drink as small as an espresso does not seem like a good value proposition, especially when paying just a bit extra will bring a much more "substantial" drink such as a latte. More to the point, most Chinese have not yet developed a taste for the coffee itself and strongly prefer their coffee beverages sweetened with milk, flavoring, or liquors. Customers ordering espresso in China are, for the most part, either foreigners or expatriates who acquired the taste in Europe or the United States.

Many of the smaller and independently owned cafés in Beijing typically exude a very intellectual feel and are located either in close proximity to universities or in places with heavy foreign foot traffic. A great example is the Bookworm, a combo bookstore and café located in an unassuming building in the embassy district. Customers can browse the books as they sip their coffees and even participate in a book exchange program. Alex Pearson, the British owner of the Bookworm who has been living in Beijing for almost two decades, organizes an annual literature festival that brings authors from around the world to several of the Bookworm's locations. The Bookworm is also a top choice for book launch parties and monthly gatherings of various special interest groups (e.g. Newcomers to Beijing). Its dedicated reading room boasts quite a collection of English, Chinese, and bilingual periodicals and books.

Several appealing cafés with a bookish feel are at the epicenter of Beijing's Silicon Alley, the area defined by the elite Tsinghua and Beijing Universities. Located inside the All Sages Bookstore, Thinker's Café boasts not only distinctive Chinese decor, but also the animated gestures, flamboyant decibels, and obligatory smoke exhalations of China's literati. Well-hidden inside a residential building complex, Space for Imagination Café often organizes premiere showings of independent films to bring its clientele together. The owners note that they are not financially motivated in running the café (their other businesses generate the "real" revenues). Rather, the lively conversations and frequent gatherings of the café's loyal patrons have become a sanctuary that balances the often neck-breaking pace of their daily lives.

For a genuine Chinese coffee chain experience, drop by any of the nine branches of Sculpting in Time (S.I.T). Several S.I.Ts are located next to universities and easily attract local students. The menu is a combination of local and Western fare. The baristas are rather knowledgeable about their coffees and preparation. The chain was founded by Jimmy Huang who is deeply immersed in the arts scene in Beijing. Originally from Taiwan, Jimmy is a graduate of the Beijing Film Academy. Together with his wife, a graduate of the Beijing Fashion Institute, he had originally planned to open a bookstore. When that hit a wall of red tape, they changed course to start a café. Unlike other chains that are strategically located in high foot traffic areas, each S.I.T. branch aims to be an oasis in an otherwise "urban desert." The locations are chosen to project a relaxed feel. In particular, patrons should be able to see greenery through the windows and be transported into a state of reflection. This design is meant to be true to the chain's namesake, the book by Russian filmmaker Andrei Tarkovsky. The title of the book, *Sculpting in Time*, refers to Tarkovsky's style of filmmaking which stands in sharp contrast to films that make strong use of rapid-cut editing and other tools. Ingmar Bergman said of the filmmaker: "*Tarkovsky for me is the greatest [director], the one who invented a new language, true to the nature of film, as it captures life as a reflection, life as a dream.*"

Any doubts about this chain's commitment to coffee quality and barista training are dispelled by visiting their training center, the well-equipped S.I.T Coffee College. There we met the chain's head trainer JinBao Lin (nicknamed Leopard) who would easily qualify for the title of Coffee Prophet of China. Leopard, who clearly consumes enough caffeine to proselytize any belief system, expounded at length about the challenges of training baristas in China, the need for exposure to more coffees and the international coffee community, and the imperative to communicate better in English. Leopard was the 2008 Chinese National Barista Champion and represented China at the World Barista Championship in Atlanta in 2009. He vows to reclaim his title and even win the world championship by 2015. He dreams of "*putting China on the world coffee map.*" He certainly makes a killer espresso, so I wouldn't count him or any of his disciples out anytime soon!

In contrast to Beijing, coffee culture in Shanghai has much deeper roots. The residents of Shanghai have long been exposed to Western influences because the city was a trading post with the West for centuries. In the early 20th century, parts of the city known as concessions were leased to foreign governments such as the French, Americans, Italians, Japanese, and Russians. During World War II, Shanghai even had a Jewish Quarter where Jews settled after escaping the wrath of the Nazis. Although most foreigners left the city after the war, strolls through the tree-lined streets of the French Concession are still evocative of that bygone era. There you will find quaint cafés ranging from the Old China Hand Reading Room with its distinctive antique furnishings and cross-cultural menu offerings, to the Coffee Tree that sports an ultramodern Western interior and LA-chic menu.

Coffee on the Roof Café, 798 Art District, Beijing

Café DeDa (founded in 1897) and its clientele exemplify the café culture and spirit of old Shanghai. If not for the predominantly Chinese patrons, upon entry you might think you just stepped into a café in Budapest or Prague. My most indelible impression of this café and of Shanghai's coffee culture was of a formally attired waiter carrying a tray with six lattes toward a table where a family of four generations was wrapping up lunch. The 89 year-old matriarch who reveled in her latte proudly told us, in impeccable English, that she is a graduate of St. John's University and has been enjoying coffee drinks since the age of 17.

While her five year-old grandson Kasper proudly and expertly packs the coffee grounds for her espresso with a tamper, seventy-something Helen Hua Ying Li gave more personal insights into the coffee culture in old Shanghai. Helen was a young child during World War II. Her first encounter with coffee was in Chongqing, when her grandfather introduced her to the brew. After they moved to Shanghai, her grandfather, who received his Ph.D. in Economics from the University of Chicago in 1917 and later became the Deputy Finance Minister in Chiang-Kai Shek's government, took her to cafés quite often. "*In those days, the atmosphere in the cafés was very different from the teahouses. People went to cafés to chat and have active exchanges with friends rather than play mahjong as they did in the teahouses.*" To be more "Western appropriate," her grandfather would instruct her to change into more formal clothing before a café outing. She happily obliged because she loved all of the pretty dresses. Because she was an unusually young patron of the cafés, the proprietors often delighted in her curiosity and patiently entertained her naive questions about Western culture and music. Helen remembers the delectable pastries well. As to coffee samples, *"what I was given more closely resembled the 'children's cappuccino' (frothed milk) that Kasper receives from you at the end of each round of espresso-making at home."*

The café culture of old Shanghai lives on today. On any given day, old-timers congregate mid-morning and mid afternoon to chat over coffee and pastries at DeDa, the Red Room, Kai Si Ling, or another one of their favorite "old" haunts. The settings of these cafés are not only evocative of Western sensibilities, but also reminiscent of the golden era of Old Shanghai when coffee first landed and café culture first flourished in China. As in those days, milk still plays a strong role in the coffee drinks of the Chinese. Analogous to the reaction of the Viennese to Turkish coffee in the late 17th century, the Chinese still like their coffees Viennese *mélange* style: the only customers at the Turkish coffee stand inside the Turkish pavilion at the 2010 Shanghai World Expo were foreigners. ✒

An 89 year-old matriarch revelling in her latte at Café DeDa, Shanghai.

798 Art District in Beijing

EPILOGUE

THE FINAL TRIP ON MY COFFEE SEARCH WAS A SYNTHESIS OF ALL THE DISCOVERIES and adventures I enjoyed during the writing of this book. The first leg took me to Greece whose coffee culture had already made an impression on me at the age of two when I sipped coffee with my Greek-born grandfather, a tradition that I still enjoy every time I visit my parents.

With my by now bountiful repertoire of coffee world insider scoop, nailing down the best café in Athens took no time. Anyone following the competitive coffee scene knows Stefanos Domatiotis of Taf Coffee in Athens. With five Greek barista champion titles under his belt, Stefanos holds more national titles in coffee than anyone else in the world and is a well-known figure on the international scene. Stefanos did not disappoint. He moved around the Taf coffee bar as if he were in a never-ending performance in front of WBC judges. He meticulously cleaned the machine and the surfaces around it, explained the characteristics of each coffee he was serving to his customers as he would in a competition, and always ensured that the patrons' tables were spotless and orderly.

Stefanos relished in exhibiting not only his technique and artistry, but also his deep knowledge about coffee. As he was preparing the Freddo, the Greek drink of choice for the summer months, he also explained with a good measure of theatrics the nuanced differences between Greek and Turkish coffee. Even though the overall coffee preparation is very similar, the Greeks traditionally use a lighter roast than the Turks and caramelize the sugar in the *ibrik* (the coffee pot) before putting in the coffee powder and bringing it to a boil. Licensing laws require that every café in Greece serve Greek coffee. Given the excellent choices of coffee offered at Taf, it is not surprising that very few of Stefanos' customers ask for it.

Chris Loukakis pouring his award-winning latte art in Maastricht.

Stefanos, with a coffee tree tattoo on his right arm, preparing a Freddo, the Greek drink of choice for summer.

I enthusiastically shared my café recommendation with 600 participants of the conference on databases that I was attending in Athens, and even devoted a portion of one of my presentations to my coffee passion. My wife and I visited Taf every day of the conference, usually joined by curious database researchers. On the day of a scheduled general strike that coincided with an IMF visit to the Greek Parliament, we had to circumvent multiple layers of police barricades to reach Taf and return to the conference in time for me to deliver a tutorial.

Stefanos is not only an iconic barista of Greece, but also a mentor and trainer for the younger generation of Greek baristas. We

Andrea Antonelli, Italy's representative, creates latte art blindfolded.

were more than delighted to meet the best example of his mentoring skills. Chris Loukakis greeted us on our first visit to Taf and introduced himself as the Latte Art Champion of Greece. Because it was the week preceding the World Latte Art Championship that was scheduled to take place in Maastricht, the Netherlands, Chris was pouring latte art at a frantic pace. We were happy to bring him a steady supply of latte art fans from the database conference. Chris practiced his beautiful artistry with every cup that came his way. In the meantime, Stefanos was gearing up for the first ever Brewer's Cup that would take place concurrently in Maastricht. Securing the national Greek championship in this category was never in question.

Needless to say, the second half of my trip was spent in Maastricht, where I joined my many coffee friends from around the world at the festivities of the World of Coffee, the venue for five coffee-themed competitions: Latte Art, Brewer's Cup, Cup Taster's, Coffee in Good Spirits, and Czeve/Ibrik. After spending a week as the "*coffee guy*" at the database conference, I relished in the seamless transition to being the "*Google guy*" at the coffee conference. In contrast to my first foray into a coffee conference two years earlier, at every turn I was greeted by friends, from farmers, importers, and roasters to world famous baristas and competition staff. I felt very much at home.

Several notable controversies arose in Maastricht. The first was over the rules for the Coffee in Good Spirits competition, where in addition to coffee and alcohol, the competitors are allowed to use any "legal" ingredient in their drinks. But here we were in the Netherlands where the notion of legal extends to substances that are proscribed elsewhere. In order to avoid impairing the sound judgment of the competition judges, the organizers demanded that the competitors stay within the much more restrictive definition of legal.

The second controversy arose in the Cup Tasters Championship where the competitors are always armed with cupping spoons and their challenge is to solve eight triangulation tests: each test includes three coffees and the task is to find which of the three is different from the other two. Speed counts to break the tie when two competitors guess the same number of correct triangulation tests. The Greek competitor Kyriakos Ouzounidis decided that it was faster to solve the triangulation tests simply by *looking* at the color differences among the cups. While this seemed like an amusing strategy during the first round and in the semifinals, controversy over the technique started to garner more attention during the finals. The finals featured Kyriakos against David Walsh from Ireland who came in second in 2010, Terukiyo Tahara from Japan (supported by his mother in the audience), and the youngest competitor ever, 19 year-old Carol Franco from Brazil whom I had the pleasure of meeting a few months earlier at the Cup of Excellence in Brazil. In a nail-biting match that came down to the very last cup, Kyriakos emerged victorious by edging out David Walsh with his speed. His winning the tasting competition by not

The bear hug: Stefanos and Chris after winning the world title in Maastricht.

JUN~~E~~ ~~2~~4, 2011
Maas~~tricht, N~~etherlands

Coffee Events

tasting at all set off a heated debate concerning the propriety of his visual technique. On the heels of the event, I had a chat with Alf Kramer, the Norwegian inventor of most of the coffee competitions. Alf asserted that next year the cups in the competition would be black (instead of white) and the lighting dim, thus returning the taster's competition to the oral realm.

The Cezve/Ibrik competition featured extremely elaborate presentations in which the competitors presented Turkish coffee and their signature drinks while sparing no effort with their table settings and equipment paraphernalia. In a sign of the changing world, Jin-Seol Bae, a Korean woman, won the competition by masterfully blending the cultures of the Far East with those of the Ottoman Empire.

The inaugural Brewers Cup attracted significant attention. It provided a stage for baristas to demonstrate their skills at hand-pouring filtered coffee techniques that have been gaining popularity in recent years but have had no representation in the competitive arena. The competition drew several baritas of world renown such as James Hoffman (the 2007 World Barista Champion) and Stefanos Domatiotis, our Greek icon. However, the unlikely winner was Keith O'Sullivan, a Ph.D. student from Ireland. Keith is a home barista who emphasized in his presentation how coffee affected his life and experiences.

The Latte Art Championship was a memorable highlight. Watching the baristas effortlessly produce intricate and gorgeous designs in the macchiatos and cappuccinos can dazzle for hours. The first round featured the Italian competitor's impressive feat of performing blindfolded without injuring himself and creating a semiprofessional design. Chris Loukakis overcame his first round jitters and regained composure as he entered the finals. After a beautifully executed and creative performance where he rocked to the rhythm of his own music, the 25 year-old barista who had served my colleagues and me in Athens a week earlier emerged as the World Latte Art Champion! The owner of Taf Coffee Yiannis Taloumis was beside himself with excitement. In his elated trance, he handed *me* his iPhone and asked me to compose the victory tweet from Taf! Stefanos the proud trainer was in tears as he bear-hugged his protégé on stage. Later that day, Greece was awarded the prize of Best Nation 2011 for best overall performance in the coffee competitions this year. These accolades brought much-needed gaiety in an otherwise turbulent economic period for the Greeks and set off an exuberant celebration that lasted well into the night.

As I wandered around the exhibit halls of the convention center in Maastricht, I could not help but marvel at the early development stage of both the specialty coffee industry and coffee culture's spread around the world. As my friend and coffee consultant Andrew Hetzel noted, you are likely to find a location ripe for further developing a coffee culture by randomly throwing a dart on the world map.

My enthralling coffee search has been deeply gratifying and tremendously rewarding. I gained a whole new level of appreciation for exquisite coffees and also innumerable friendships in this close-knit community. I am delighted to be able to share with you the highlights of my journey through the coffee tales in this travelogue. Above all, I have come to realize that my initial search is only the overture to a lifelong coffee serenade of infinite emotions around the globe. ✍

Costa Rica

Bosnia

At home

China

Brazil

London

ACKNOWLEDGMENTS

Writing this book was an eye-opening experience. It has been a pleasure and a privilege to cross paths with many amazing coffee professionals from around the world without whom I would not be able to share these personal stories.

I started the project with nothing but the chutzpah to cold-email people in the coffee business. Thankfully, it did not take long for me to be able to approach any coffee professional with the implicit backing of mutual Facebook friends and to become a welcomed member of the coffee community. I owe thanks to my worldwide network of computer science colleagues who proved to be well-connected to their local coffee communities.

Much like the book itself, my acknowledgments are organized by geography.

Ethiopia

Ethiopia was the penultimate stop on my world tour because I felt it needed the most preparation. By the time I came around to organizing the trip, I had already become a fine-tuned coffee traveling machine. My visit to Ethiopia was carefully orchestrated by Donna Sillan and Tsegaye Beleke who run Common River from Mill Valley in California. Even as I sat in a traditional Sidama hut in Aleta Wondo, my local host's cell phone had rung with Tsegaye verifying that everything was running smoothly. Tsegaye had nothing to worry about. I was in the excellent hands of Fisseha Cherenet and his wife Almaz who hosted me from the minute I landed in Addis Ababa to the moment I left. Fisseha drove me down to Sidama and took care of my every need during the trip. Almaz prepared the most delectable Ethiopian meal I ever had upon our return to Addis. During our visit to Common River in Aleta Wondo, the head of the school and his staff showed warm hospitality.

I was introduced to Donna and Tsegaya by Willem Boot, an international coffee expert whom I accosted after a coffee-related presentation he gave in Berkeley, California. I must thank Andrew Barnett and Kent Bakke for pointing me Willem's way.

Europe

Researching coffee in Europe required six separate trips. Given its important role in coffee history, Vienna was one of the first destinations. The highlight of the trip with my wife was our visit to Cafe Hawelka where we interviewed Leopold Hawelka and his son Gunter. My computer science network made the interview possible. I first heard about the Hawelkas during a casual conversation with Christoph Koch, an Austrian who is currently a professor at Ecole Polytechnique Fédérale de Lausanne. When he saw my eyes light up, he embarked on a long series of phone calls that required every bit of Austrian cultural knowhow. To ensure a smooth interview, Christoph even arranged for his colleague from Vienna, Professor Reinhard Pichler, to serve as interpreter. Georg Gottlob, another Austrian colleague who is currently a professor at Oxford University, equipped me with a list of must-visit cafés in Vienna. Anno Langen, a member of my team at Google, provided a critical factoid about coffee in Germany by tipping me off to Tchibo. My wife and I thoroughly enjoyed visiting a Tchibo shop in the heart of Vienna where she delighted in modeling with coffee and lingerie in hand.

In Prague, we were fortunate to run into a local university student Lenka Zelena at Café Montmartre. I had heard about the poem written about Café Slavia by the Czech Nobel Laureate Jaroslav Seifert. However, I was at a complete loss to track down the poem. Lenka not only found the poem but also provided its English translation that appears in the book.

Raghu Ramakrishnan from Yahoo! was kind enough to tour the historic cafés of Paris with me after a long flight from the U.S. I owe Raghu and all my Indian friends an apology for not including a chapter on India. I promise to make up for the omission in a future edition. I had the pleasure of exploring some of the lesser-known cafés of Paris with my second cousin Daphna Alshech.

In London, Anette Moldvaer and James Hoffmann of Square Mile Coffee graciously hosted me at their roastery where I enjoyed my first ever macchiato prepared by a former World Barista Champion. Grant Rattray, the executive director of Alliance for Coffee Excellence (the organization that runs the Cup of Excellence) filled me in on other coffee-related aspects of the city as we rode together to coffee farms in Brazil. Gwilym Davies kindly entertained my many other questions on the several occasions I was fortunate to meet him.

The task of writing about coffee in Italy was, to put it mildly, intimidating. I was incredibly fortunate to meet Vinko Sandalj, the owner of Sandalj Coffee Company and a walking encyclopedia of coffee knowledge who was the then head of the coffee association of Trieste. Vinko graciously hosted me in Trieste and gave me a comprehensive primer on Italian coffee culture. The introduction to

Vinko was triggered by my offhand comment during a keynote talk that I gave in Florida, after which Tsvi Kuflik from the University of Haifa introduced me to his colleague Oliviero Stock, a college buddy of Vinko. Oliviero Stock also took me to the best ice cream shop in Trieste, a refreshing break from cafés. Lorenzo Martinelli, one of the friends I made on my Cup of Excellence trip to Brazil, filled me in on other Italian coffee trivia such as the caffe sospeso. A former colleague from the University of Washington, Gaetano Borriello, was tasked with the cultural experiment of ordering a macchiatone in Naples. He was brushed away with the accusatio—"is that another American invention?"

This book project provided a great excuse to revisit Scandinavia, one of my favorite parts of the world. Ylva Lillberg, whom I met over a really bad cup of coffee in Plzen, Czech Republic, convinced me that I should definitely visit Sweden during my world coffee tour. She proved her point by showing me around the nice spots of Stockholm and some wonderful cafés. She also guided me to my first experience at a Swedish fika. Hanna Zuring, a Dutch woman living in Stockholm whom I found accidentally through a blog, tipped me off to cafés in both Sweden and the Netherlands. Anne Lunell of Koppi Coffee in Helsingborg, Camilla Pettersson and Per Nordby of DaMatteo, and Eva Nordell from Are Koffiteri rounded out my Swedish coffee knowledge.

In Copenhagen, Linus Törsäter was a gracious host at the Coffee Collective. His wife Yara Thais, the two-time barista champion of Brazil, helped me complete my caffeinated visit to Copenhagen at Estate Coffee. My colleague Christian Jensen, a professor of computer science at Aarhus University, was a never-ending source of coffee information about Denmark (though we still disagree about the merits for darker roasts). Together with Fritz Storm, the 2002 World Barista Champion, Christian helped me figure out the coffee scene in Copenhagen.

My spare no effort devotion to the coffee project reached a crescendo when I ventured to Oslo on a cold February day to visit Tim Wendelboe, a former World Barista Champion. It was well worth the special trip because I learned so much from him! While in Oslo, I also enjoyed visiting with Robert Thoresen, the first World Barista Champion, and his cafes.

I met the Ferrer family during the World Barista Championship in London and asked if I could write their story for my book. Their reaction was: "Sure, come visit us in Reykjavík," which seemed completely logical given the circumstances. Sonja Grant was an awesome host who took me around the city. Carlos Ferrer and his wife Yrsa hosted me for an evening at their summerhouse near the town of Selfoss. The evening with all the Ferrers, including Ingibjörg, Tumi and their significant others, was truly unforgettable.

When I started the book, Bosnia was not on my radar for a coffee related visit. I resisted taking the bait after a conversation with Geoffrey King at Ritual Cafe in San Francisco during which he clued me in on the special Bosnian coffee culture. When a waiter at Café Central in Vienna told me his story about buying coffee in Sarajevo, I finally caved. Nadya Ivanova, a Bulgarian student in Chicago whom I got to know through my colleague Carl Ganter, introduced me to Lejla Djuric, a law student from Bosnia. Lejla immediately began to send my way a plethora of stories, anecdotes and videos relating to coffee culture in Bosnia. I spent three wonderful days with Lejla and her twin brother Zeljko in Sarajevo. We sampled an incredible variety of Bosnian food and cafés, and I also received an intensive course on Bosnian politics. Lejla also tipped me to the coffee cup installation by Aida Sehovic. I met Aida in New York, where she had just completed a degree in Art. She gave me the background on her coffee project. This chapter was published in modified form in the February/March 2011 edition of *Barista Magazine*.

In Greece, I simply could not get enough of Taf Coffee. In fact, I went there every single day of my stay in Athens. Stefanos Domitoitis and Chris Loukakis were great hosts and shared their coffee knowledge and beautiful latte art designs with me, my wife, and my computer science colleagues who joined us for café outings. I would also like to thank Stefanos, Chris and Taf's owner, Yiannis Taloumis for sharing with me the jubilation a week later in Maastricht, when Chris won the Latte Art World Championship.

I made several trips to Israel during the coffee search. My infatuation with coffee had taken my parents Moshe and Dvora Levy by surprise at the outset of the project as they thought I had turned into a rather odd computer scientist. But my parents and sister Sharona Levy were indulgent. They accompanied me on my café excursions. My father arranged a visit with Pnina and Israel Shar'abi, where I learned about Yemenite coffee traditions. My niece Danielle Menuhin, who had been working at the local Arcaffe near my hometown, gave me a glimpse of barista life in Israel.

I was introduced to Ariel Rubinstein by two professors, Yoav Shoham, a computer science professor at Stanford, and Hal Varian, an economist from Berkeley who is currently the Chief Economist at Google. Ariel's advice about cafés in Tel Aviv and New York was invaluable to me. I was also inspired by the passion that a renowned scientist like him had found in the world of cafés. I would like to thank Ariel and Ayelet Dekel for allowing me to include the translation of Ariel's article about the University of Cafés. Sara Shemer gave me a fascinating description of how she founded one of the most successful café chains in Israel. Jonathan Kidon, a son of one of Sara's previous business partners and one of my former interns at Google, introduced me to her.

Asia and the Pacific

I first met Emily Oak through one of her *Barista Magazine* articles. Emily not only gave me excellent advice before my trip Down Under, hosted me most thoughtfully in Sydney, but also kept introducing me to other coffee professionals around the world and answering my random questions. Jason Scheltus of Market Lane Coffee, Bridget Amor of Seven Seeds, and Andrew Kelly of The Auction Rooms helped wrap my brain around the lively café scene in Melbourne. Nolan Hirte of Proud Mary showed me the technical prowess of a coffee tinkerer. Sonya Bennett and Greg Peacok made my visit to Brisbane a total pleasure. I look forward to returning to visit their new café, Stomp Espresso. Alan Fekete, a University of Sydney computer science professor endowed with terrific culinary skills, took me on my first visit to an espresso machine factory.

South Korea was one of the biggest surprises during my coffee search. JongHoon Lee gave me a fascinating and very caffeinated tour of Seoul. He explained in great detail the subtle aspects of Korean coffee culture. Yunson Lee of Terarosa Coffee helped shed light on a few important details. Nailing down JongHoon's contact information had been rather tricky because the Korean web is organized in mysterious ways. Ultimately, I had to rely on my Korean computer science network. Stephen Whang, a Korean Ph.D. student at Stanford, came to the rescue and provided all the details that enabled me to connect with Barista Hoon.

Lior Nuchi, a lawyer whom I met through my wife, tipped me off to Barry Eisler's books about Tokyo's café culture. My trip to Tokyo ended up being organized around Barry's café suggestions posted on his web site. Andrea Calì, an Italian computer science colleague, accompanied me to some of these cafés and in true Italian style, made theatrical remarks about the contrast between Japanese and Italian coffee cultures. Over an amazing shot of single-origin espresso from Bolivia at Maruyama Coffee, Mie Nakahara gave me the lowdown on the Japanese specialty coffee scene. I'd like to thank Miki Suzuki for allowing me to include her awesome card from the 2011 WBC in the book.

My visit to China was preceded by a month-long café-related intelligence gathering and field research performed by my wife Oriana, a native of Beijing. By the time I arrived, we went straight to the bull's eyes by visiting with café owners and baristas who were at the forefront of China's emerging coffee culture. Among the most informative were the folks at the training center of Sculpting in Time (in particular, Jinbao Lin, a former Chinese barista champion) and Alex Pearson, the owner of The Bookworm Cafe. My mother-in-law, Helen Li, gave me a sentimental account of the 1940's café scene in Shanghai.

Central and South America

Roukiat Delrue qualifies as the best friend suggestion Facebook ever gave me. When she is not on a plane (which is rare), Rouki lives in Guatemala and is the coordinator for all the coffee competitions in the Americas. Rouki entertained my seemingly innumerable questions about coffee with great patience. Her introductions to key people paved the way for my fruitful trip to Central America that included Costa Rica, Guatemala and El Salvador. It was a special treat to share the drive with Rouki and Raul Rodas from Guatemala City to Santa Ana, El Salvador.

In Costa Rica, I was hosted by Roberto Mata, the amazingly inspiring general manager of Coope Dota. Roberto spent hours taking me around the farms, explaining not only the coffee processes but also the social aspects of the cooperative, and hosting me at his home for a real taste of Costa Rica. William Rojas was extremely kind during and after my visit. He even managed to help me fit in a quick tour of some of Costa Rica's tourist highlights on the way back to the airport. My colleagues Brad Zlotnik, Dan Janzen, and Winnie Hallwachs who spend much of their time in Costa Rica regularly sent me interesting coffee related stories about that country. Carl Ganter provided me the opportunity to dine with Costa Rica's former president, José-Maria Figueres.

In Guatemala, I could not have asked for a better host than Raul Rodas who had recently won second place in the 2010 World Barista Championship. During the memorable week that I spent with Raul, he drove me to some of the most distinctive farms in Guatemala and introduced me to farmers he knew well. Enio Perez, Raul Perez, and Mauricio Rosales made my visits to their farms unforgettable (special thanks to Mauricio's wife who sent sandwiches that served as our delicious breakfast at La Maravilla). Rouki, Raul and I made a most memorable trip down to El Salvador, where Aida Batlle and Mario Mendoza-Corleto hosted us at her guesthouse and told us all we needed to know about coffee in El Salvador. I would like to thank Brent Fortune for being the first to alert me about the drama surrounding Raul's performance in Atlanta in 2009 and Ruben Sagastume for a quick introduction to coffee in El Salvador.

At the invitation of Grant Rattray and Jon Lewis of Alliance for Coffee Excellence to be an observer for the CoE jury, I attended my very first CoE event in Brazil in November 2010. It was an absolute pleasure to be immersed 24 hours a day with coffee folks and learn so much about the processing and tasting of coffee. Silvio Leite, one of the pioneers of specialty coffee in Brazil, gave me an illuminating background of the origins of the specialty movement in the world's largest coffee producing nation and of the competitions that originated there. Marco Suplicy provided a spirited café experience in one of his cafés in São Paulo. Georgia Franco and her daughter Carol enthralled me one of the most personal stories about the coffee industry in Brazil and taught me a thing or two about cupping coffee while they were at it. Coffee consultant John Thompson from Edinburgh, Scotland made sure that all the questions about coffee processing that I was too shy to ask anyone else were answered, and Michael de Renouard was very generous with his photos from the trip.

The chapter on Colombia was written after numerous discussions with Hector Gonzalez, a Colombian research scientist on my team at Google and a grandson of a coffee farmer. As I was discovering the world of coffee, it was refreshing to have frequent conversations (at the espresso machine, of course) with someone who grew up breathing coffee culture.

The United States

The United States chapter was one of the most challenging to write. Andrew Barnett was my anchor for questions and introductions to other coffee professionals in the U.S. and worldwide. Based in San Francisco, he had to endure my more frequent visits and a few lunches at Google headquarters. He was incredibly generous with his time and even gave me a quick cupping course in his house before we headed off to the Cup of Excellence in Brazil together. The couple of hours I spent with George Howell over lunch in San Francisco were of the most eye opening in the entire process. George has an uncanny ability to summarize complex ideas with pithy comments. During my CoE trip to Brazil, I gained more perspective about the Howell family after meeting his daughter Jenny, the director of coffee at George Howell Coffee.

Peter Giuliano and Geoff Watts provided broader perspectives and keen insights on the global specialty coffee industry and the evolution of direct trade in the last decade. They also helped untangle the complex topic of coffee sustainability. Ric Reinhard, the CEO of the Specialty Coffee Association of America, outlined the challenges facing the coffee industry today. Susie Spindler, one of the founders of the CoE, shed light on the coffee climate in the United States leading up to the founding of the CoE. David Schomer and Kent Bekke supplied very colorful accounts and anecdotes on the coffee scene in Seattle. Kris Engskov, a Vice President at Starbucks, shared insights about his employer. Greg Sherwood took me to Caffe Trieste in San Francisco and graphically recounted the atmosphere there in the 1950s and 1960s that he experienced as the son of one of the major spokespeople for the Beatnik movement.

I was most fortunate to spend quality time with quite a few of the amazing American baristas, including the 2010 World Barista Champion Mike Phillips, Nick Griffith who hosted me at Intelligentsia in Silver Lake, M'lissa Owens at the other Intelli in Venice Beach, Tal Mor and Zachary Carlsen at Four Barrel in San Francisco, Ben Kaminsky from Ritual, Amber Fox of Ecco Café, Andy Sprenger of Caffe Pronto, Sarah Peterson who founded the Abbey Café in Santa Cruz before she joined Verve, Nick Cho and Trish Rothgeb who moved to the Bay Area just in time to help round out my coffee education, and Kyonghee Shin who gave me and my family a crash course on the different methods of drip coffee. Andrew Hetzel, the man who keeps the world's airlines in business by constantly flying to remote destinations from his hub in Hawaii, was always quick to answer my random questions, whether or not coffee related. I am indebted to Emily Rocke, a Google colleague who was the first to bring to my attention the concept of barista competitions and made the initial introductions to that crowd.

I owe special thanks to Sarah Allen and Ken Olson, the editors of *Barista Magazine*, for their many invaluable tips. In addition to the wealth of information contained in every issue of their periodical, they were generous with introductions and photos.

I thank Amanda Wilson, who was introduced to me by Sarah Allen, for the terrific design of the book. In addition to her creativity and painstaking attention to details that would have never crossed my mind, Amanda went above and beyond the call of duty to collect coffee related photographs from around the world and embarked on a few special missions in the Pacific Northwest to fill critical gaps with her own photography.

Gianni Cassatini embodies the spirit of the coffee community. From the very first moment our paths crossed at the 2009 U.S.

Barista Championship in Portland, Gianni has made me feel at home in the coffee community. On several occasions his effusiveness truly made my day. The Gianni T-shirt is, of course, priceless!

As a first-time author of a nontechnical book, I had many questions about the writing and publishing business. Katie Hafner graciously provided guidance and introductions. Carl Ganter was always generous with advice and introductions and constantly supplied me wonderful photography as he trotted the globe furthering the important mission of the Circle of Blue. I'm grateful to the following people for their advice at various stages of the book project: James Levine, Michaele Weismann, David Elliot Cohen, Michael Adelberg, Amanda Edmonds, Lauren Nemroff. I would like to thank Geralyn Peterkin, Oriana's high school English teacher, for providing feedback on a very early draft of the manuscript.

Home Base

I was fortunate to receive much essential information from home base in the Silicon Valley. My team at Google that includes a grandson of a Colombian coffee farmer, a former owner of café in Seoul, and a son of a longtime employee of Hills Brothers Coffee, always humored my coffee antics and related travel. My manager Alfred Spector was a good sport who graciously put up with my coffee addiction (and even used it to his advantage on occasion). Mike Cafarella, a former Ph.D. advisee and Google intern who is currently on the faculty of the University of Michigan, consistently forwarded me coffee-related articles.

Last, but certainly not least, I would like to thank my wife Oriana who shared intimately in this book as a work in progress. Thanks to my in-laws Helen Li and Paul Jing, Oriana and I had the opportunity to explore many cafés together. A corporate attorney and certified interpreter by training and translator by avocation, Oriana edited and improved the book through multiple drafts with the skills, discipline, precision and dedication of a professional editor. Her constant barrage of insightful questions prompted more thorough research at critical junctures and made the final product greater in its scope of coverage, richer in details, and more compelling in its storytelling. Her marvelous facility with words and intense passion for the expressive art of writing infused eloquence, animation and emotional depth into the narrative. Without Oriana's contributions, readers would be entitled to conclude that I was at best fueled by decaf throughout this journey. I dedicate this book to her and to Karina and Kasper, our pride and joy.

REFERENCES

As this is not aimed at being a scholarly undertaking, I have avoided the use of footnotes and stayed clear of mentioning sources in the body of the text. Several sources for historical facts and many interviews for more recent data informed the research of this book. They are organized by book section below.

Origins of Coffee
The most detailed account of coffee's early history in Ethiopia, the Ottoman Empire and its spread around the globe is from [19]. Additional background is in [12], [16] and [9]. An amusing account of the history of coffee is in [2]. The more recent data about Ethiopia are from [13] and personal communications with Donna Sillan, Tsegaye Bekele, and my hosts in Ethiopia.

Europe
Details concerning the arrival and acceptance of coffee in Europe are from [12], [16] and [9], with [2] providing an entertaining account of the same events. Some of the landmark cafes of Europe, their famous patrons, and their history are detailed in [10]. The trading scene in Amsterdam in the early 17th century is described vividly in the novel [11].

Details on the contemporary café scene in London were gleaned from conversations with James Hoffmann, Anette Moldvaer, Gwilym Davies and Grant Rattray. The history of Cafe Hawelka is based on interviewing Gunter Hawelka. Translation credit of the poem by Jaroslav Seifert goes to Lenka Zelena.

The account of Italian coffee benefited tremendously from a lengthy interview with Vinko Sandalj and some historical background from [12]. Tim Wendelboe contributed greatly to my description of coffee in Scandinavia. The information about Iceland comes from Sonja Grant, Carlos Ferrer, Ingibjörg Ferrer and Tumi Ferrer. The chapter on Bosnia is based on extensive interviews with Lejla Djuric, Zeljko Djuric and Aida Sehovic. The chapter on Israel was based on interviews with Ariel Rubinstein and Pnina Shar'abi, Sarah Shemer and, of course, informed by 25 years of living in Israel.

The United States
A detailed description of the history of coffee in the United States appears in [12]. The chapter on San Francisco benefited from interviews with Andrew Barnett and Greg Sherwood. The chapter on Seattle was shaped by interviews with David Schomer and Kent Bekke and eight years of living in the city. The chapter on Starbucks was greatly informed by [4]. The remainder of the section benefited from interviews with George Howell, Geoff Watts, Mike Phillips, Peter Giuliano, Nick Griffith, Sarah Allen, Trish Rothgeb and Nick Cho.

Sound and Central America
Before venturing to South and Central America I read a comprehensive account of the region's history of coffee there from [12]. The chapter on Guatemala is based on interviews with Raul Rodas, Roukiat Delrue and the owners of the farms we visited. The chapter on El Salvador is based on interviewing Aida Batlle and [19]. The story of Coope Dota is based on an interview with Roberto Mata. The chapter on Colombia was helped by discussions with Hector Gonzalez. The chapter on Brazil was greatly informed by [12] and interviews with Georgia and Carolina Franco, Marco Suplicy, Andrew Barnett, and Silvio Leite. For basic knowledge about coffee processing and roasting I turned to [7] and [18].

Asia and the Pacific
The chapter on Australia is based on many discussions with Emily Oak and the owners of the cafes I visited. Many of the cafes I visited in Tokyo were inspired by [8]. The chapter on Korea is based on daylong interview with Lee JongHoon as we visited the cafes of the city. The chapter on China was made possible by extensive research by my wife Oriana Halevy and benefited from interviews with JinBao Lin and Helen Li.

The World

It would be impossible to list all the people who impacted this section of the book. My description of the Cup of Excellence was greatly influenced by conversations with Susie Spindler, Grant Rattray, Jon Lewis and Silvio Leite and George Howell. Several books ([6], [14], [15]) detailing various coffee drinks helped whet my appetite for globe trotting.

1.   Sarah Allen. *Trip Report from El Salvador*. Barista Magazine, April/May 2011.
2.   Stewart Lee Allen. *The Devil's Cup: A History of the World According to Coffee*. Ballantine Books, 1999.
3.   Dawn Campbell and Janet Smith. *The Coffee Book*. Pelican Publishing Company Inc., 1993.
4.   Taylor Clark. *Starbucked: A Double Tall Tale of Caffeine, Commerce, and Culture*. Little Brown and Company, Hachette Book Group. 2007.
5.   A.K. Crump, Kristen Jensen, P. Segal. *The Cafes of San Francisco*. TCB-Cafe Publishing, 2009.
6.   Kenneth Davids. *Espresso: Ultimate Coffee*. St. Martin Griffin's Publisher, 2001.
7.   Fulvio Eccardi and Vincenzo Sandalj. *Coffee: A Celebration of Diversity*. Redacta, S.A. de C.V Publishers. 2000.
8.   Barry Eisler. *Rain Fall*. Penguin Books, 2003.
9.   Markman Ellis. *The Coffee House, a Cultural History*. Wiedenfeld & Nicolson, 2004.
10. Noel Riley Fitch. *The Grand Literary Cafes of Europe*. New Holland, 2006.
11. David Liss. *The Coffee Trader*. Random House, 2003.
12. Mark Pendergrast. *Uncommon Grounds: The History of Coffee and How it Transformed Our World*. Basic Books, 1999.
13. David Pohl. *Field Report: Ethiopia*. Barista Magazine, February/March 2011.
14. Jon Thorn. *The Coffee Companion: A connoisseur's Guide*. (updated by Michael Segal). Running Press, 2006.
15. Michael Turback. *Mocha*. The Speed Press, 2007.
16. Bennett Alan Weinberg and Bonnie K. Bealer. *The World of Caffeine: The Science and Culture of the World's Most Popular Drug*. Routledge Taylor & Francis Group, 2001.
17. Michaele Weissman. *God in a Cup— The Obsessive Quest for the Perfect Coffee*. Wiley, 2008.
18. Tim Wendelboe. *Coffee with Tim Wendelboe*. Schibsted Forlag. 2010
19. Anthony Wile. *Coffee, A Dark History*. W. W. Norton and Company, New York, 2004.

PHOTOGRAPHY CREDITS

I would like to thank many friends and colleagues who generously contributed photos to the book. They are listed below by page number. All other photos are from my personal collection.

Cover
(right) Amanda Wilson

Contents
(second and fifth) J. Carl Ganter; (third) Amanda Wilson

Preface
J. Carl Ganter (2)

The World of Coffee
8-9: Amanda Wilson
10: (top) Amanda Wilson; (bottom) courtesy of Liz Clayton
11: (diagram) Amanda wilson
12: (top) Amanda Wilson
13: (left) Amanda Wilson; (right) Anette Moldvaer
16: Michael de Renouard
18: (top) Michael de Renouard
20: Amanda Wilson
22-23: Sad Giraffe (3)
26: Courtesy of *Barista Magazine*
27: Created with *Google Fusion Tables*
28: Shawn Collins
30: Created with *Google Insights for Search*

The Origins of Coffee
39: Donna Sillan
43: (map) Amanda Wilson

Europe
44: Amanda Wilson
58-59: Peter Norvig
68: (top) Aida Šehović
72: (bottom) Robert Fink
73: Craig Nevill-Manning
74: Amanda Wilson
75: Courtesy of Anette Moldvaer
76: (top) Courtesy James Hoffman; (bottom) Amanda Wilson
78: Courtesy of Tim Wendelboe
80: (right top & bottom) J. Carl Ganter (2)
84: (top) Héöinn Eiríksson

The United States of America
90-91: Amanda Wilson
94: (charts) Amanda Wilson
97: (top) Amanda Wilson
99: (top) Courtesy of David Schomer; (bottom) Amanda Wilson
100: (bottom) Mark Munden/La Marzocco
101: Amanda Wilson
102: (left) Amanda Wilson; (right) David Reamer
103: (top) Amanda Wilson
105: Courtesy of George Howell (2)
106: (bottom) Michael de Renouard
107: (left) Amanda Wilson; (right) J. Carl Ganter
108: Courtesy of DrinkEatTravel.com

South and Central America
110-111: Amanda Wilson
112: Courtesy of *Barista Magazine*
120: (top) Aida Batlle
123-125: Amanda Wilson (4)
129: Courtesy of Marco Suplicy

Asia and the Pacific Rim
130: Amanda Wilson
132: Bridget Amor
135: (left) Coutesy of Sonya Bennett and Greg Pocock
139: (bottom) Amanda Wilson; Card courtesy of Miki Suzuki

Epilogue
148: (left) Robert Berner

Back Cover
Amanda Wilson

Back Flap
Oriana Halevy